Everybody's Guide to the Internet

Everybody's Guide to the Internet

Adam Gaffin

The MIT Press
Cambridge, Massachusetts
London, England

This book was set in Palatino by DEKR Corporation and was printed and bound in the United States of America.

Library of Congress Cataloging-in-Publication Data

Gaffin, Adam.
  Everybody's guide to the internet / Adam Gaffin.
    p. cm.
  Includes index.
  ISBN 0-262-57105-6
  1. Internet (Computer network) I. Title.
TK5105.875.I57G34 1994
384.3—dc20   94-7083
                                                                CIP

Contents

Foreword

Welcome to the world of the Internet.

The Electronic Frontier Foundation (EFF) is proud to have sponsored the production of *Everybody's Guide to the Internet*. EFF is a nonprofit organization based in Washington, D.C., dedicated to ensuring that everyone has access to the newly emerging communications technologies vital to active participation in the events of our world. As more and more information is available online, new doors open up for those who have access to that information. Unfortunately, unless access is broadly encouraged, individuals can be disenfranchised and doors can close, as well. *Everybody's Guide to the Internet* was written to help open some doors to the vast amounts of information available on the world's largest network, the Internet.

The spark for *Everybody's Guide to the Internet*, and its companion electronic version, *EFF's Guide to the Internet*, was ignited in a few informal conversations that included myself and Steve Cisler of Apple Computer, Inc., in June of 1991. With the support of Apple Computer, EFF engaged Adam Gaffin to write the book and actually took on the project in September of 1991. The guide was originally published electronically in July of 1993 as the *Big Dummy's Guide to the Internet*.

The idea was to write a guide to the Internet for people who had little or no experience with network communications. We intended to post this guide to the net in ASCII and HyperCard formats and to give it away on disk, as well as have a print edition available. We have more than realized our goal. Individuals from as geographically far away as Germany, Italy, Canada, South Africa, Japan, Scotland, Norway, and Antarctica have all sent electronic mail to say that they downloaded the guide. *Everybody's Guide to the Internet* is now available in a wide array of formats, including ASCII text, HyperCard,

World-Wide Web, PostScript, and AmigaGuide. And the guide is finally available in a printed format, as well.

You can find the electronic version of *Everybody's Guide to the Internet* by using anonymous ftp to ftp.eff.org and accessing pub/Net_info/Guidebooks/EFF_Net_Guide/netguide.eff. Or send an e-mail message to info@eff.org. The electronic version is entitled *EFF's Guide to the Internet* and is updated on a regular basis.

EFF would like to thank author Adam Gaffin for doing a terrific job of explaining the Net in such a nonthreatening way. We'd also like to thank the folks at Apple, especially Steve Cisler of the Apple Library, for their support of our efforts to bring this guide to you. Finally, we'd like to thank our publishers at MIT Press, especially Bob Prior, for working out an arrangement with us where we can continue to distribute the text in electronic format and forego our royalties in order to keep the price of the book low.

We invite you to join with EFF in our fight to ensure that equal access to the networks and free speech are protected in newly emerging technologies. We are a membership organization, and through donations like yours, we can continue to sponsor important projects to make communications easier. Information about the Electronic Frontier Foundation and some of the work that we do can be found at the end of this book.

We hope that *Everybody's Guide to the Internet* helps you learn about whole new worlds, where new friends and experiences are sure to be yours. Enjoy!

Mitchell Kapor
Chairman of the Board
Electronic Frontier Foundation
mkapor@eff.org

For comments, questions, or requests regarding EFF or *Everybody's Guide to the Internet*, send a note to ask@eff.org.

Preface

Welcome to the Internet! You're about to start a journey through a unique land without frontiers, a place that is everywhere at once— even though it exists physically only as a series of electrical impulses. You'll be joining a growing community of millions of people around the world who use this global resource on a daily basis.

With this book, you will be able to use the Internet to

• stay in touch with friends, relatives, and colleagues around the world, at a fraction of the cost of phone calls or even air mail;

• discuss everything from archaeology to zoology with people in several different languages;

• tap into thousands of information databases and libraries worldwide;

• retrieve any of thousands of documents, journals, books, and computer programs;

• stay up-to-date with wire-service news and sports and with official weather reports;

• play live, "real-time" games with dozens of other people at once.

Connecting to "the Net" today takes something of a sense of adventure, a willingness to learn, and an ability to take a deep breath every once in a while. Visiting the Net is a lot like journeying to a foreign country. There are so many things to see and do, but everything at first will seem so, well, foreign.

When you first arrive, you won't be able to read the street signs. You'll get lost. If you're unlucky, you may even run into some locals who'd just as soon you went back to where you came from. As if this weren't enough, the entire country is constantly under construction; every day, it seems like there's something new for you to figure out.

Fortunately, most of the locals are actually friendly. In fact, the Net has a rich tradition of helping out visitors and newcomers. Until very recently, there were few written guides for ordinary people, and the Net grew largely through an "oral" tradition in which the old-timers helped the newcomers.

So when you connect, don't be afraid to ask for help. You'll be surprised at how many people will lend a hand!

Without such folks, in fact, this guide would not be possible. My thanks to all the people who have written with suggestions, additions, and corrections since the guide (originally titled *Big Dummy's Guide to the Internet*) first appeared on the Internet in 1993.

Special thanks go to my loving wife, Nancy. I would also like to thank the following people, who, whether they know it or not, provided particular help: Rhonda Chapman, Jim Cocks, Tom Czarnik, Christopher Davis, David DeSimone, Jeanne deVoto, Phil Eschallier, Nico Garcia, Joe Granrose, Ronda Hauber, Joerg Heitkoetter, Joe Ilacqua, Jonathan Kamens, Peter Kaminski, Thomas A. Kreeger, Stanton McCandlish, A. Richard Miller, Leanne Phillips, Nancy Reynolds, Helen Trillian Rose, Barry Shein, Jennifer "Moira" Smith, Gerard van der Leun, and Scott Yanoff.

If you have any suggestions or comments on how to make this guide better, I'd love to hear them. You can reach me via e-mail at adamg@world.std.com.

Everybody's Guide to the Internet

1

Setting Up and Jacking In

1.1 Ready, Set . . .

The world is just a phone call away. With a computer and modem, you'll be able to connect to the Internet, the world's largest computer network (and if you're lucky, you won't even need the modem; many colleges and companies now give their students or employees direct access to the Internet).

The phone line can be your existing voice line—just remember that if you have any extensions, you (and everybody else in the house or office) won't be able to use them for voice calls while you are connected to the Net.

A modem is a sort of translator between computers and the phone system. It's needed because computers and the phone system process and transmit data, or information, in two different and incompatible ways. Computers "talk" digitally; that is, they store and process information as a series of discrete numbers. The phone network relies on analog signals, which on an oscilloscope would look like a series of waves. When your computer is ready to transmit data to another computer over a phone line, your modem converts the computer numbers into these waves (the conversion sounds like a lot of screeching)—it "modulates" them. In turn, when information waves come into your modem, it converts them into numbers your computer can process, by "demodulating" them.

Increasingly, computers come with modems already installed. If yours didn't, you'll have to decide what speed of modem to get. Modem speeds are judged in "bps rate" or bits per second. One bps means the modem can transfer roughly one bit per second; the greater the bps rate, the more quickly a modem can send and receive information. A letter or character is made up of eight bits.

You can now buy a 2400-bps modem for well under $60—and most now come with the ability to handle fax messages as well. At prices that now start around $150, you can buy a modem that can transfer data at 14,400 bps (and often even faster, using special compression techniques). If you think you might be using the Net to transfer large numbers of files, a faster modem is always worth the price. It will dramatically reduce the amount of time your modem or computer is tied up transferring files and, if you are paying for Net access by the hour, will save you quite a bit in online charges.

Like the computer to which it attaches, a modem is useless without software to tell it how to work. Most modems today come with easy-to-install software. Try the program out. If you find it difficult to use or understand, consider a trip to the local software store to find a better program. You can spend several hundred dollars on a communications program, but unless you have very specialized needs, this will be a waste of money, as there are a host of excellent programs available for around $100 or less. Among the basic features you want to look for are a choice of different "protocols" (more on them in a bit) for transferring files to and from the Net and the ability to write "script" or "command" files that let you automate such steps as logging into a host system.

When you buy a modem and the software, ask the dealer how to install and use them. Try out the software if you can. If the dealer can't help you, find another dealer. You'll not only save yourself a lot of frustration, you'll also have practiced the prime Internet directive: "Ask. People know."

To fully take advantage of the Net, you must spend a few minutes going over the manuals, or documentation, that come with your software. There are a few things you should pay special attention to: uploading and downloading, screen capturing (sometimes called "screen dumping"), logging, how to change protocols, and terminal emulation. It is also essential to know how to convert a file created with your word-processing program into "ASCII" or "text" format, which will let you share your thoughts with others across the Net.

Uploading is the process of sending a file from your computer to a system on the Net. Downloading is retrieving a file from somewhere on the Net to your computer. In general, things in cyberspace go "up" to the Net and come "down" to you.

Chances are your software will come with a choice of several "protocols" to use for these transfers. These protocols are systems designed to ensure that line noise or static does not cause errors that could ruin whatever information you are trying to transfer. Essentially, when using a protocol, you are transferring a file in a series of pieces. After each piece is sent or received, your computer and the Net system compare it. If the two pieces don't match exactly, they transfer it again, until they agree that the information they both have is identical. If, after several tries, the information just doesn't make it across, you'll either get an error message or your screen will freeze. In that case, try it again. If, after five tries, you are still stymied, something is wrong with (a) the file, (b) the telephone line, (c) the system you're connected to, or (d) your own computer.

From time to time, you will likely see messages on the Net that you want to save for later viewing—a recipe, a particularly witty remark, something you want to write your congressman about, whatever. This is where screen capturing and logging come in.

When you tell your communications software to capture a screen, it opens a file in your computer (usually in the same directory or folder used by the software) and "dumps" an image of whatever happens to be on your screen at the time.

Logging works a bit differently. When you issue a logging command, you tell the software to open a file (again, usually in the same directory or folder as used by the software) and then give it a name. Then, until you turn off the logging command, everything that scrolls on your screen is copied into that file, sort of like recording on videotape. This is useful for capturing long documents that scroll for several pages—using screen capture, you would have to repeat the same command for each new screen.

Terminal emulation is a way for your computer to mimic, or emulate, the way other computers put information on the screen and accept commands from a keyboard. In general, most systems on the Net use a system called VT100. Fortunately, almost all communications programs now on the market support this system as well—make sure yours does.

You'll also have to know about protocols. There are several different ways for computers to transmit characters. Fortunately, there are only two protocols that you're likely to run across: 8-1-N (which stands for "8 bits, 1 stop bit, no parity"—yikes!) and 7-1-E (7 bits, 1 stop bit, even parity).

In general, many Unix-based systems use 7-1-E, while MS-DOS-based systems use 8-1-N. What if you don't know what kind of system you're connecting to? Try one of the settings. If you get what looks like gobbledygook when you connect, you may need the other setting. If so, you can either change the setting while connected and then hit enter, or hang up and try again with the other setting. It's also possible your modem and the modem at the other end can't agree on the right bps rate. If changing the protocols doesn't work, try using another bps rate (but no faster than the one listed for your modem). Don't worry, you can't break anything! If something looks wrong, it probably is wrong. Change your settings and try again. Nothing is learned without trial, error, and effort.

There are the basics. Now on to the Net!

1.2 Go!

Once, only people who studied or worked at an institution directly tied to the Net could connect to the world. Today, though, an ever-growing number of "public-access" systems provide access for everybody. These systems can now be found in several states, and there are a couple of sites that can provide access across the country.

There are two basic kinds of these host systems. The more common one is known as a UUCP site (UUCP being a common way to transfer information among computers using the Unix operating system) and offers access to international electronic mail and conferences.

However, recent years have seen the growth of more powerful sites that let you tap into the full power of the Net. These Internet sites not only give you access to electronic mail and conferences but to such services as databases, libraries, and huge file and program collections around the world. They are also fast—as soon as you finish writing a message, it gets zapped out to its destination.

Some sites are run by for-profit companies; others by nonprofit organizations. Some of these public-access, or host, systems are free of charge. Others charge a monthly or yearly fee for unlimited access. And a few charge by the hour. Systems that charge for access will usually let you sign up online with a credit card. Some also let you set up a billing system.

But cost should be only one consideration in choosing a host system, especially if you live in an area with more than one provider. Most systems let you look around before you sign up. What is the range of each of their services? How easy is each one to use? What kind of support or help can you get from the system administrators?

The last two questions are particularly important because many systems provide no user interface at all; when you connect, you are dumped right into the Unix operating system. If you're already familiar with Unix, or you want to learn how to use it, these systems offer phenomenal power—in addition to Net access, most also let you tap into the power of Unix to do everything from compiling your own programs to playing online games.

But if you don't want to have to learn Unix, there are other public-access systems that work through menus (just like the ones in restaurants; you are shown a list of choices and then you make your selection of what you want), or which provide a "user interface" that is easier to figure out than the ever-cryptic Unix.

If you don't want or need access to the full range of Internet services, a UUCP site makes good financial sense. These sites tend to charge less than commercial Internet providers, although their messages may not go out as quickly.

Some systems also have their own unique local services, which can range from extensive conferences to large file libraries.

1.3 Public-Access Internet Providers

When you have your communications program dial one of these host systems, one of two things will happen when you connect. You'll either see a lot of gibberish on your screen, or you'll be asked to log in. If you see gibberish, chances are you have to change your software's parameters (to 7–1-E or 8–1-N as the case may be). Hang up, make the change, and then dial in again.

When you've connected, chances are you'll see something like this:

```
Welcome to THE WORLD
Public Access UNIX for the '90s
Login as 'new' if you do not have an account

login:
```

That last line is a prompt asking you to do something. Since this is your first call, type

```
new
```

and hit enter. Often, when you're asked to type something by a host system, you'll be told what to type in quotation marks (for example, 'new'). Don't include the quotation marks. Repeat: Don't include the quotation marks.

What you see next depends on the system but will generally consist of information about costs and services (you might want to turn on your communication software's logging function, to save this information). You'll likely be asked if you want to establish an account now or just look around the system.

You'll also likely be asked for your "user name." This is not your full name but a one-word name you want to use while online. It can be any combination of letters or numbers, all in lower case. Many people use their first initial and last name (for example, "jdoe"); their first name and the first letter of their last name (for example, "johnd"); or their initials ("jxd"). Others use a nickname. You might want to think about this for a second, because this user name will become part of your electronic-mail address (see chapter 2 for more on that). The one exception is the various Free-Net systems, all of which assign you a user name consisting of an arbitrary sequence of letters and numbers.

You are now on the Net. Look around the system. See if there are any help files for you to read. If it's a menu-based host system, choose different options just to see what happens. Remember: You can't break anything. The more you play, the more comfortable you'll be.

What follows is a list of public-access Internet sites, which are computer systems that offer access to the Net. All offer international e-mail and Usenet (international conferences). In addition, they offer the following:

FTP: File-transfer protocol—access to hundreds of file libraries (everything from computer software to historical documents to song lyrics). You'll be able to transfer these files from the Net to your own computer.

Telnet: Access to databases, computerized library card catalogs, weather reports, and other information services, as well as live, online games that let you compete with players from around the world.

Additional services that may be offered include the following:

WAIS: Wide-Area Information Server; a program that can search dozens of databases in one search.

Gopher: A program that gives you easy access to hundreds of other online databases and services by making selections on a menu. You'll also be able to use these to copy text files and some programs to your mailbox.

IRC: Internet Relay Chat, a CB simulator that lets you have live keyboard chats with people around the world.

However, even on systems that do not provide these services directly, you will be able to use a number of them through telnet (see chapter 6). In the list that follows, systems that let you access services through menus are noted; otherwise assume that when you connect, you'll be dumped right into Unix (the operating system sometimes known as MS-DOS with a college degree). Several of these sites are available nationwide through national data networks such as the CompuServe Packet Network and SprintNet.

Please note that all listed charges are subject to change. Many sites require new or prospective users to log on a particular way on their first call; this list provides the name you'll use in such cases.

Alabama

Huntsville. Nuance. Call the following voice number for modem number. $35 setup fee; $25 a month. Voice: (205) 533-4296.

Alaska

Anchorage. University of Alaska Southeast, Tundra Services, (907) 789-1314; has local dial-in service in several other cities. $20 a month. Voice: (907) 465-6453.

Alberta

Edmonton. PUCNet Computer Connections, (403) 484-5640. Log on as: guest. $0 setup fee; $25 for 20 hours a month plus $6.25 an hour for access to ftp and telnet. Voice: (403) 448-1901.

Arizona

Phoenix/Tucson. Internet Direct, (602) 274-9600 (Phoenix); (602) 321-9600 (Tucson). Log on as: guest. $20 a month. Voice: (602) 274-0100 (Phoenix); (602) 324-0100 (Tucson).

Tucson. Data Basics, (602) 721-5887. $25 a month or $180 a year. Voice: (602) 721-1988.

British Columbia

Victoria. Victoria Free-Net, (604) 595-2300. Menus. Access to all features requires completion of a written form. Users can "link" to other Free-Net systems in Canada and the United States. Free. Log on as: guest. Voice: (604) 389-6026.

California

Berkeley. Holonet. Menus. For free trial, modem number is (510) 704-1058. For information or local numbers, call the voice number. $60 a year for local access, $2 an hour during off-peak hours. Voice: (510) 704-0160.

Cupertino. Portal. Both Unix and menus. (408) 725-0561 (2400 bps); (408) 973-8091 (9600/14,400 bps). $19.95 setup fee, $19.95 a month. Voice: (408) 973-9111.

Irvine. Dial N' CERF. See San Diego.

Los Angeles/Orange County. Kaiwan Public Access Internet, (714) 539–5726; (310) 527-7358. $15 signup; $11 a month (credit card). Voice: (714) 638-2139.

Los Angeles. Dial N' CERF. See San Diego.

Oakland. Dial N' CERF. See San Diego.

Pasadena. Dial N' CERF. See San Diego.

Palo Alto. Institute for Global Communications, (415) 322-0284. Unix. Local conferences on environmental/peace issues. Log on as: new. $10 a month and $3 an hour after first hour. Voice: (415) 442-0220.

San Diego. Dial N' CERF USA. Run by the California Education and Research Federation. Provides local dial-up numbers in San Diego, Los Angeles, Oakland, Pasadena, and Irvine. For more information, call voice (800) 876-CERF or (619) 534-5087. $50 setup fee; $20 a month plus $5 an hour ($3 on weekends). Voice: (800) 876-2373.

San Diego. CTS Network Services, (619) 637-3660. Log on as: help. $15 set-up fee, monthly fee of $10 to $23 depending on services used. Voice: (619) 637-3637.

San Diego. Cyberspace Station, (619) 634-1376. Unix. Log on as: guest. $10 sign-up fee; $15 a month or $60 for six months.

San Francisco. Pathways. Call voice number for modem number. Menus. $25 setup fee; $8 a month and $3 an hour. Voice: (415) 346-4188.

San Jose. Netcom, (510) 865-9004 or 426-6610; (408) 241-9760; (415) 424-0131, up to 9600 bps. Unix. Maintains archives of Usenet postings. Log on as: guest. $15 startup fee and then $17.50 a month for unlimited use if you agree to automatic billing of your credit-card account (otherwise $19.50 a month for a monthly invoice). Voice: (408) 554-UNIX.

San Jose. A2i, (408) 293-9010. Log on as: guest. $20 a month; $45 for three months; $72 for six months.

Sausalito. The Whole Earth 'Lectronic Link (WELL), (415) 332-6106. Uses moderately difficult Picospan software, which is sort of a cross between Unix and a menu system. New users get a written manual. More than two hundred WELL-only conferences. Log on as: newuser. $15 a month plus $2 an hour. Access through the nationwide Compu-Serve Packet Network available for another $4.50 an hour. Voice: (415) 332-4335. Recorded message about the system's current status: (800) 326-8354 (continental United States only).

Colorado

Colorado Springs/Denver. CNS, (719) 570-1700 (Colorado Springs); (303) 758-2656 (Denver). Local calendar listings and ski and stock reports. Users can choose between menus or Unix. Log on as: new. $35 setup fee; $2.75 an hour (minimum fee of $10 a month). Voice: (719) 592-1240.

Colorado Springs. Old Colorado City Communications, (719) 632-4111. Log on as: newuser. $25 a month. Voice: (719) 632-4848.

Denver. Denver Free-Net, (303) 270-4865. Menus. Access to all services requires completion of a written form. Users can "link" to other Free-Net systems across the country. Free. Log on as: guest.

Golden. Colorado SuperNet. Unix. E-mail to fax service. Available only to Colorado residents. Local dial-in numbers available in several Colorado cities. For dial-in numbers, call the voice number. $3 an hour ($1 an hour between midnight and 6 A.M.); one-time $20 sign-up fee. Voice: (303) 273-3471.

Delaware

Middletown. Systems Solutions, (302) 378-1881. $20 setup fee; $25 a month for full Internet access. Voice: (800) 331-1386.

Florida

Talahassee. Talahassee Free-Net, (904) 488-5056. Menus. Full access requires completion of a registration form. Can "link" to other Free-Net systems around the country. Voice: (904) 488-5056.

Georgia

Atlanta. Netcom, (303) 758-0101. See Los Angeles, California, for information on rates.

Illinois

Champaign. Prarienet Free-Net, (217) 255-9000. Menus. Log on as: visitor. Free for Illinois residents; $25 a year for others. Voice: (217) 244-1962.

Chicago. MCSNet, (312) 248-0900. $25/month or $65 for three months of unlimited access; $30 for three months of access at 15 hours a month. Voice: (312) 248-UNIX.

Peoria. Peoria Free-Net, (309) 674-1100. Similar to Cleveland Free-Net (see Ohio). Users can "link" to the larger Cleveland system for access to Usenet and other services. There are also Peoria Free-Net public-access terminals in numerous area libraries, other government buildings, and senior-citizen centers. Contact the voice number for specific locations. Full access (including access to e-mail) requires completion of a written application. Free. Voice: (309) 677-2544.

Maryland

Baltimore. Express Access, (410) 766-1855; (301) 220-0462; (714) 377-9784. Log on as: new. $20 setup fee; $25 a month or $250 a year. Voice: (800) 969-9090.

Baltimore. Clarknet, (410) 730-9786; (410) 995-0271; (301) 596-1626; (301) 854-0446. Log on as: guest. $23 a month, $126 for six months or $228 a year. Voice: (410) 730-9765.

Massachusetts

Bedford. The Internet Access Company, (617) 275-0331. To log on, follow online prompts. $20 setup fee; $19.50 a month. Voice: (617) 275-2221.

Brookline. The World, (617) 739-9753. "Online Book Initiative" collection of electronic books, poetry, and other text files. Log on as: new. $5 a month plus $2 an hour or $20 for 20 hours a month. Available nationwide through the CompuServe Packet Network for another $5.60 an hour. Voice: (617) 739-0202.

Lynn. North Shore Access, (617) 593-4557. Log on as: new. $10 for 10 hours a month; $1 an hour after that. Voice: (617) 593-3110.

Worcester. NovaLink, (508) 754-4009. Log on as: info. $12.95 sign-up fee (includes first two hours); $9.95 a month (includes five daytime hours), $1.80 an hour after that. Voice: (800) 274-2814.

Michigan

Ann Arbor. MSEN. Contact number below for dial-in number. $20 setup fee; $20 a month. Voice: (313) 998-4562.

Ann Arbor. Michnet. Has local dial-in numbers in several Michigan numbers. For local numbers, call the voice number. $35 a month plus one-time $40 sign-up fee. Additional network fees for access through non-Michnet numbers. Voice: (313) 764-9430.

New Hampshire

Manchester. MV Communications, Inc. For local dial-up numbers call the voice number. $5 a month mininum plus variable hourly rates depending on services used. Voice: (603) 429-2223.

New Jersey

New Brunswick. Digital Express, (908) 937-9481. Log on as: new. $20 setup fee; $25 a month or $250 a year. Voice: (800) 969-9090.

New York

New York. Panix, (212) 787-3100. Unix or menus. Log on as: newuser. $40 setup fee; $19 a month or $208 a year. Voice: (212) 877-4854.

New York. Echo, (212) 989-8411. Unix, but with local conferencing software. Log on as: newuser. $19.95 ($13.75 students and seniors) a month. Voice: (212) 255-3839.

New York. MindVox, (212) 989-4141. Local conferences. Log on as: guest. $10 setup fee for non-credit-card accounts; $15 a month. Voice: (212) 989-2418.

New York. Pipeline, (212) 267-8606 (9600 bps and higher); (212) 267-7341 (2400 bps). Offers graphical interface for Windows for $90. Log on as: guest. $20 a month and $2 an hour after first 20 hours or $35 a month unlimited hours. Voice: (212) 267-3636.

New York. Maestro, (212) 240-9700. Log on as: newuser. $12 a month or $140 a year. Voice: (212) 240-9600.

North Carolina

Charlotte. Vnet Internet Access, (704) 347-8839; (919) 406-1544. Log on as: new. $25 a month. Voice: (704) 374-0779.

Triangle Research Park. Rock Concert Net. Call voice number for local modem numbers in various North Carolina cities. $30 a month; one-time $50 sign-up fee. Voice: (919) 248-1999.

Ohio

Cleveland. Cleveland Free-Net, (216) 368-3888. Ohio and U.S. Supreme Court decisions, historical documents, many local conferences. Full access (including access to e-mail) requires completion of a written application. Free. Voice: (216) 368-8737.

Cincinnati. Tri-State Free-Net, (513) 579-1990. Similar to Cleveland Free-Net. Full access (including access to e-mail) requires completion of a written application. Free.

Cleveland. Wariat, (216) 481-9436. Unix or menus. $20 setup fee; $35 a month. Voice: (216) 481-9428.

Dayton. Freelance Systems Programming, (513) 258-7745. $20 setup fee; $1 an hour. Voice: (513) 254-7246.

Lorain. Lorain County Free-Net, (216) 277-2359 or 366-9753. Similar to Cleveland Free-Net. Users can "link" to the larger Cleveland system for additional services. Full access (including access to e-mail) requires completion of a written application. Free.Voice: (216) 366-4200.

Medina. Medina Free-Net, (216) 723-6732, 225-6732, or 335-6732. Users can "link" to the larger Cleveland Free-Net for additional services. Full access (including access to e-mail) requires completion of a written application. Free.

Youngstown. Youngstown Free-Net, (216) 742-3072. Users can "link" to the Cleveland system for services not found locally. Full access (including access to e-mail) requires completion of a written application. Free.

Ontario

Ottawa. National Capital FreeNet, (613) 780-3733 or (613)564-3600. Free, but requires completion of a written form for access to all services.

Toronto. UUNorth. Call voice number for local dial-in numbers. $20 startup fee; $25 for 20 hours a month of off-peak use. Voice: (416) 225-8649.

Toronto. Internex Online, (416) 363-3783. Both Unix and menus. $40 a year for one hour a day. Voice: (416) 363-8676.

Oregon

Beaverton. Techbook, (503) 220-0636 (2400 bps); (503) 220-1016 (higher speeds). $10 a month for 30 hours of "basic" Internet access or $90 a year; $15 a month for 30 hours of "deluxe" access or $150 a year. $10 sign-up fee for monthly accounts.

Portland. Agora, (503) 293-1772 (2400 bps), (503) 293-2059 (9600 bps or higher). Log on as: apply. $6 a month for one hour per day.

Portland. Teleport, (503) 220-0636 (2400 bps); (503) 220-1016 (9600 and higher). Log on as: new. $10 a month for one hour per day. Voice: (503) 223-4245.

Pennsylvania

Pittsburgh. Telerama, (412) 481-5302. $6 for 10 hours a month, 60 cents for each additional hour. Voice: (412) 481-3505.

Quebec

Montreal. Communications Accessibles Montreal, (514) 931-7178 (9600 bps); (514) 931-2333 (2400 bps). $25 a month. Voice: (514) 931-0749.

Rhode Island

East Greenwich. IDS World Network, (401) 884-9002. In addition to Usenet, has conferences from the Fidonet and RIME networks. $10 a month; $50 for six months; $100 for a year.

Providence/Seekonk. Anomaly, (401) 331-3706. $125 for six months or $200 a year. Educational rate of $75 for six months or $125 a year. Voice: (401) 273-4669.

Texas

Austin. RealTime Communications, (512) 459-4391. Log on as: new. $75 a year. Voice: (512) 451-0046.

Dallas. Texas Metronet, (214) 705-2901; (817) 261-1127. Log on as: info or signup. $10 to $35 setup fee, depending on service; $10 to $45 a month, depending on service. Voice: (214) 705-2900 or (817) 543-8756.

Houston. The Black Box, (713) 480-2686. $21.65 a month. Voice: (713) 480-2684.

United Kingdom

London. Demon Internet Systems, 44 (0)81 343 4848. £12.50 setup fee; £10 a month or £132.50 a year. Voice: 44 (0)81 349 0063.

Virginia

Norfolk/Peninsula. Wyvern Technologies, (804) 627-1828 (Norfolk); (804) 886-0662 (Peninsula). $10 startup fee; $15 a month or $144 a year. Voice: (804) 622-4289.

Washington (State)

Seattle. Halcyon, (206) 382-6245. Users can choose between menus and Unix. Log on as: new. $10 setup fee; $60 a quarter or $200 a year. Voice: (206) 955-1050.

Seattle. Eskimo North, (206) 367-3837 (all speeds), (206) 362-6731 (9600/14.4K bps). $10 a month or $96 a year. Voice: (206) 367-7457.

Washington, D.C.

The Meta Network. Call voice number for local dial-in numbers. Caucus conferencing, menus. $15 setup fee; $20 a month. Voice: (703) 243-6622.

CapAccess, (202), 784-1523. Log on as guest with a password of visitor. A Free-Net system (see Cleveland, Ohio, for information). Free. Voice: (202) 994-4245.

See also Baltimore, Maryland, for Express Access and Clarknet.

1.4 If Your Town Has No Direct Access

If you don't live in an area with a public-access site, you'll still be able to connect to the Net. Several of these services offer access through national data networks such as the CompuServe Packet Network and SprintNetz, which have dozens, even hundreds, of local dial-in numbers across the country. These include Holonet in Berkeley, California; Portal in Cupertino, California; the WELL in Sausalito, California; Dial 'N CERF in San Diego, California; the World in Brookline, Massachusets; and Michnet in Ann Arbor, Michigan. Dial 'N CERF offers access through an 800 number. Expect to pay from $2 to $12 an hour to use these networks, above each provider's basic charges. The exact amount depends on the network, time of day, and type of modem you use. For more information, contact the individual services.

Four other providers deliver Net access to users across the country:

Delphi, based in Cambridge, Massachusetts, is a consumer-oriented network much like CompuServe or America Online—only it now offers subscribers access to Internet services. Delphi charges $3 a month for Internet access, in addition to standard charges. These are $10 a month for four hours of off-peak (nonworking hours) access a month and $4 an hour for each additional hour or $20 for 20 hours of access a month and $1.80 an hour for each additional hour. For more information, call (800) 695-4005.

BIX (the Byte Information Exchange) offers ftp, telnet, and e-mail access to the Internet as part of their basic service. Owned by the same company as Delphi, it also offers 20 hours of access a month for $20. For more information, call (800) 695-4775.

PSI, based in Reston, Virginia, provides nationwide access to Internet services through scores of local dial-in numbers to owners of IBM and compatible computers. PSILink, which includes access to e-mail, Usenet, and ftp, costs $29 a month, plus a one-time $19 registration fee. Special software is required but is available free from PSI. PSI's Global Dialup Service provides access to telnet for $39 a month plus a one-time $39 set-up fee. For more information, call (800) 82PSI82 or (703) 620-6651.

NovX Systems Integration, based in Seattle, Washington, offers full Internet access through an 800 number reachable across the United States. There is a $24.95 setup fee, in addition to a monthly fee of $19.95 and a $10.50 hourly charge. For more information, call (206) 447-0800.

1.5 Net Origins

In the 1960s, researchers began experimenting with linking computers to each other and to people through telephone hookups, using funds from the U.S. Defense Department's Advanced Research Projects Agency (ARPA).

ARPA wanted to see if computers in different locations could be linked using a new technology known as packet switching. This technology, in which data meant for another location is broken up into little pieces, each with its own "forwarding address," had the promise of letting several users share just one communications line. Just as important, from ARPA's viewpoint, was that this allowed for creation of networks that could automatically route data around downed circuits or computers. ARPA's goal was not the creation of today's international computer-using community but development of a data network that could survive a nuclear attack.

Previous computer networking efforts had required a line between each computer on the network, sort of like a one-track train route. The packet system allowed for creation of a data highway, in which large numbers of vehicles could essentially share the same lane. Each packet was given the computer equivalent of a map and a time stamp so that it could be sent to the right destination, where it would then be reassembled into a message the computer or a human could use.

This system allowed computers to share data and the researchers to exchange electronic mail, or e-mail. In itself, e-mail was something of a revolution, offering the ability to send detailed letters at the speed of a phone call.

As this system, known as ARPANet, grew, some enterprising college students (and one in high school) developed a way to use it to conduct online conferences. These started as science-oriented discussions, but they soon branched out into virtually every other field, as people recognized the power of being able to "talk" to hundreds, or even thousands, of people around the country.

In the 1970s, ARPA helped support the development of rules, or protocols, for transferring data between different types of computer networks. These "internet" (from "internetworking") protocols made it possible to develop the worldwide Net we have today that links all sorts of computers across national boundaries. By the close of the 1970s, links developed between ARPANet and counterparts in other countries. The world was now tied together in a computer web.

In the 1980s, this network of networks, which became known collectively as the Internet, expanded at a phenomenal rate. Hundreds, then thousands, of colleges, research companies, and government agencies began to connect their computers to this worldwide Net. Some enterprising hobbyists and companies unwilling to pay the high costs of Internet access (or unable to meet stringent government regulations for access) learned how to link their own systems to the Internet, even if "only" for e-mail and conferences. Some of these systems began offering access to the public. Now anybody with a computer and modem—and persistence—could tap into the world.

In the 1990s, the Net continues to grow at exponential rates. Some estimates are that the volume of messages transferred through the Net grows 20 percent a month. In response, government and other users have tried in recent years to expand the Net itself. Once, the main Net "backbone" in the United States moved data at 56,000 bits per second. That proved too slow for the ever-increasing amounts of data being sent over it, and in recent years the maximum speed was increased to 1.5 million and then 45 million bits per second. Even before the Net was able to reach that latter speed, however, Net experts were already figuring out ways to pump data at speeds of up to 2 billion bits per second—fast enough to send the entire Encyclopedia Britannica across the country in just one or two seconds. Another major change has been the development of commercial services that provide internetworking services at speeds comparable to those of the government system. In fact, by mid-1994, the U.S. government will remove itself from any day-to-day control over the workings of the Net, as regional and national providers continue to expand.

1.6 How It Works

The worldwide Net is actually a complex web of smaller regional networks. To understand it, picture a modern road network of trans-continental superhighways connecting large cities. From these large cities come smaller freeways and parkways to link together small towns, whose residents travel on slower, narrow residential ways.

The Net superhighway is the high-speed Internet. Connected to this are computers that use a particular system of transferring data at high speeds. In the United States, the major Internet "backbone" theoreti-cally can move data at rates of 45 million bits per second (compare this to the average home modem, which has a top speed of roughly 9,600 to 14,400 bits per second).

Connected to the backbone computers are smaller networks serving particular geographic regions, which generally move data at speeds around 1.5 million bits per second.

Feeding off these in turn are even smaller networks or individual computers.

Unlike commercial networks such as CompuServe or Prodigy, the Internet is not run by one central computer or computers—its re-sources are to be found among thousands of individual computers. This is both its greatest strength and its greatest weakness. The ap-proach means it is virtually impossible for the entire Net to crash at once—even if one computer shuts down, the rest of the network stays up. The design also reduces the costs for an individual or organization to get onto the network. But thousands of connected computers can also make it difficult to navigate the Net and find what you want—especially as different computers may have different commands for plumbing their resources. It is only recently that Net users have begun to develop the sorts of navigational tools and "maps" that will let neophytes get around without getting lost.

Nobody really knows how many computers and networks actually make up this Net. Some estimates say there are now as many as five thousand networks connecting nearly 2 million computers and more than 15 million people around the world. Whatever the actual numbers, however, it is clear they are only increasing.

The Net is more than just a technological marvel. It is human communication at its most fundamental level. The pace may be a little quicker when the messages race around the world in a few seconds, but it's not much different from a large and interesting party. You'll see things in cyberspace that will make you laugh; you'll see things that will anger you. You'll read silly little snippets and new ideas that make you think. You'll make new friends and meet people you wish would just go away.

Major network providers continue to work on ways to make it easier for users of one network to communicate with those of another. Work is under way on a system for providing a universal "white pages" in which you could look up somebody's electronic-mail address, for example. This trend toward connectivity will likely speed up in coming years as users begin to demand seamless network access, much as telephone users can now dial almost anywhere in the world without worrying about how many phone companies actually have to connect their calls.

And today, the links grow ever closer between the Internet and such commercial networks as CompuServe and Prodigy, whose users can now exchange electronic mail with their Internet friends. Some commercial providers, such as Delphi and America Online, are working to bring their subscribers direct access to Internet services. And as it becomes easier to use, more and more people will join this worldwide community we call the Net.

Being connected to the Net takes more than just reading conferences and logging messages to your computer; it takes asking and answering questions, exchanging opinions—getting involved. If you chose to go forward, to use and contribute, you will become a citizen of cyberspace. If you're reading these words for the first time, this may seem like an amusing but unlikely notion—that one could "inhabit" a place without physical space. But put a mark beside these words. Join the Net and actively participate for a year. Then reread this passage. It will no longer seem so strange to be a "citizen of cyberspace." It will seem like the most natural thing in the world.

And that leads to a fundamental thing to remember:

You can't break the Net!

As you travel the Net, your computer may freeze, your screen may erupt into a mass of gibberish. You may think you've just disabled a million-dollar computer somewhere—or even your own personal computer. Sooner or later, this feeling happens to everyone—and likely more than once. But the Net and your computer are hardier than you think, so relax. You can no more break the Net than you can the phone system. If something goes wrong, try again. If nothing at all happens, you can always disconnect. If worse comes to worst, you can turn off your computer. Then take a deep breath. And dial right back in. Leave a note for the person who runs the computer to which you've connected to ask for advice. Try it again. Persistence pays.

Stay and contribute. The Net will be richer for it—and so will you.

1.7 When Things Go Wrong

• Your computer connects with a public-access site, and you get gibberish on your screen.

If you are using parameters of 8-1-N, try 7-1-E (or vice-versa). If that doesn't work, try another modem speed.

• You have your computer dial a public-access site, but nothing happens.

Check the phone number you typed in. If it's correct, turn on your modem's speaker (on Hayes-compatible modems, you can usually do this by typing ATM1 in your communications software's "terminal mode"). If the phone just rings and rings, the public-access site could be down for maintenance or due to a crash or some other problem. If you get a "connect" message but nothing else, try hitting enter or escape a couple of times.

• You try to log in, but after you type your password, nothing happens, or you get a "timed-out" message followed by a disconnect.

Re-dial the number and try it again.

• Always remember, if you have a problem that just doesn't go away, ask! Ask your system administrator, ask a friend, but ask. Somebody will know what to do.

1.8 FYI

The Net grows so fast that even the best guide to its resources would be somewhat outdated the day it was printed. At the end of each chapter, however, you'll find FYI ("For Your Information") pointers to places on the Net where you can go for more information or to keep updated on new resources and services.

One of those resources is Everybody's Update to the Internet. Every month, this free electronic newsletter will update you on new Net services and resources. Look for it in Usenet's alt.internet.services conference (see chapter 3) and on the Electronic Frontier Foundation's ftp archive site (see chapter 7).

Peter Kaminski maintains a list of systems that provide public access to Internet services. It's availble on the network itself, which obviously does you little good if you currently have no access, but which can prove invaluable should you move or want to find a new system. Look for his "PDIAL" file in the alt.bbs.lists or news.answers newsgroups in Usenet (for information on accessing Usenet, see chapter 3).

Steven Levy's book *Hackers: Heroes of the Computer Revolution* (Anchor Press/Doubleday, 1984). describes the early culture and ethos that ultimately resulted in the Internet and Usenet.

John Quarterman's *The Matrix: Computer Networks and Conferencing Systems Worldwide* (Digital Press, 1990) is an exhaustive look at computer networks and how they connect with each other.

You'll find numerous documents about the Internet, its history, and its resources in the pub/Net_info directory on the Electronic Frontier Foundation's ftp server (see chapter 7 to decipher this).

2 E-Mail

2.1 The Basics

Electronic mail, or e-mail, is your personal connection to the world of the Net. All of the millions of people around the world who use the Net have their own e-mail addresses. A growing number of "gateways" tie more and more people to the Net every day. When you logged onto the host system you are now using, it automatically generated an address for you, as well.

The basic concepts behind e-mail parallel those of regular mail. You send mail to people at their particular addresses. In turn, they write to you at your e-mail address. You can subscribe to the electronic equivalent of magazines and newspapers. You might even get electronic junk mail.

E-mail has two distinct advantages over regular mail. The most obvious is speed. Instead of several days, your message can reach the other side of the world in hours, minutes, or even seconds (depending on where you drop off your mail and the state of the connections between there and your recipient). The other advantage is that once you master the basics, you'll be able to use e-mail to access databases and file libraries. You'll see how to do this later, along with learning how to transfer program and data files through e-mail.

E-mail also has advantages over the telephone. You send your message when it's convenient for you. Your recipients respond at their convenience. No more telephone tag. And while a phone call across the country or around the world can quickly result in huge phone bills, e-mail lets you exchange vast amounts of mail for only a few pennies—even if the other person is in New Zealand.

E-mail is your connection to help—your Net lifeline. The Net can sometimes seem a frustrating place! No matter how hard you try, no matter where you look, you just might not be able to find the answer to whatever is causing you problems. But when you know how to use e-mail, help is often just a few keystrokes away: you can ask your system administrator or a friend for help in an e-mail message.

The quickest way to start learning e-mail is to send yourself a message. Most public-access sites actually have several different types of mail systems, all of which let you both send and receive mail. We'll start with the simplest one, known, appropriately enough, as "mail," and then look at a couple of other interfaces. At your host system's command prompt, type

```
mail username
```

where username is the name you gave yourself when you first logged on. Hit enter. The computer might respond with

```
subject:
```

Type

```
test
```

or, actually, anything at all (but you'll have to hit enter before you get to the end of the screen). Hit enter.

The cursor will drop down a line. You can now begin writing the actual message. Type a sentence, again, anything at all. And here's where you hit your first Unix frustration, one that will bug you repeatedly: you have to hit enter before you get to the very end of the line. Just like typewriters, many Unix programs have no word wrapping (although there are ways to get some Unix text processors, such as emacs, to word wrap).

When done with your message, hit return. Now hit control-D (the control and the D keys at the same time). This is a Unix command that tells the computer you're done writing and that it should close your "envelope" and mail it off (you could also hit enter once and then, on a blank line, type a period at the beginning of the line and hit enter again).

You've just sent your first e-mail message. And because you're sending mail to yourself, rather than to someone somewhere else on the Net, your message has already arrived, as we'll see in a moment.

If you had wanted, you could have even written your message on your own computer and then uploaded it into this electronic "envelope." There are a couple of good reasons to do this with long or involved messages. One is that once you hit enter at the end of a line in "mail" you can't readily fix any mistakes on that line (unless you use some special commands to call up a Unix text processor). Also, if you are paying for access by the hour, uploading a prepared message can save you money. Remember to save the document in ASCII or text format. Uploading a document you've created in a word processor that uses special formatting commands (which these days means many programs) will cause strange effects.

When you get that blank line after the subject line, upload the message using the ASCII protocol. Or you can copy and paste the text, if your software allows that. When done, hit control-D as before.

Now you have mail waiting for you. Normally, when you log on, your public-access site will tell you whether you have new mail waiting. To open your mailbox and see your waiting mail, type

```
mail
```

and hit enter.

When the host system sees "mail" without a name after it, it knows you want to look in your mailbox rather than send a message. Your screen, on a plain-vanilla Unix system, will display this:

```
Mail version SMI 4.0 Mon Apr 24 18:34:15 PDT 1989
   Type ? for help.
"/usr/spool/mail/adamg": 1 message 1 new 1 unread

>N 1 adamg    Sat Jan 15 20:04  12/290  test
```

Ignore the first line; it's just computerese of value only to the people who run your system. You can type a question mark and hit return, but unless you're familiar with Unix, most of what you'll see won't make much sense at this point.

The second line tells you the directory on the host system where your mail messages are put, which again, is not something you'll likely need to know. The second line also tells you how many messages are in your mailbox, how many have come in since the last time you looked, and how many messages you haven't read yet.

It's the third line that is of real interest—it tells you who the message is from, when it arrived, how many lines and characters it takes up, and what the subject is. The "N" means it is a new message—it arrived after the last time you looked in your mailbox. Hit enter. And there's your message—only now it's a lot longer than what you wrote!

```
Message 1:
From adamg Jan 15 20:04:55 1994
Received: by eff.org id AA28949
(5.65c/IDA-1.4.4/pen-ident for adamg); Sat, 15 Jan 1994
20:04:55-0400
(ident-sender: adamg@eff.org)
Date: Sat, 15 Jan 1994 21:34:55 -0400
From: Adam Gaffin <adamg>
Message-Id: <199204270134.AA28949@eff.org>
To: adamg
Subject: test
Status: R
This is only a test!
```

Whoa! What is all that stuff? It's your message with a postmark gone mad. Just as the postal service puts its marks on every piece of mail it handles, so do Net postal systems. Only it's called a "header" instead of a postmark. Each system that handles or routes your mail puts its stamp on it. Since many messages go through a number of systems on their way to you, you will often get messages with headers that seem to go on forever. Among other things, a header will tell you exactly when a message was sent and received (even the difference between your local time and Greenwich Mean Time—as at the end of the fourth line in this message).

If this had been a long message, it would just keep scrolling across and down your screen—unless the people who run your public-access site have set it up to pause every 24 lines. One way to deal with a message that doesn't stop is to use your telecommunication software's logging or text-buffer function. Start it before you hit the number of the message you want to see. Your computer will ask you what you want to call the file you're about to create. After you name the file and hit enter, type the number of the message you want to see and hit enter. When the message finishes scrolling, turn off the text-buffer function. The message is now saved in your computer. This way, you can read the message while not connected to the Net (which can save you money if you're paying by the hour) and write a reply offline.

But in the meantime, now what? You can respond to the message, delete it, or save it. To respond, type a lowercase r and hit enter. You'll get something like this:

```
To: adamg
Subject: Re: test
```

Note that this time, you don't have to enter a user name. The computer takes it from the message you're replying to and automatically addresses your message to its sender. The computer also automatically inserts a subject line, by adding "Re:" to the original subject. From here, it's just like writing a new message. But say you change your mind and decide not to reply after all. How do you get out of the message? Hit control-C once. You'll get this:

```
(Interrupt—one more to kill letter)
```

If you hit control-C once more, the message will disappear and you'll get back to your mail's command line.

Now, if you type a lowercase d and then hit enter, you'll delete the original message. Type a lowercase q to exit your mailbox.

If you type a q without first hitting d, your message is transferred to a file called mbox. This file is where all read but undeleted messages go. If you want to leave it in your mailbox for now, type a lowercase x and hit enter. This gets you out of mail without making any changes.

The mbox file works a lot like your mailbox. To access it, type

```
mail -f mbox
```

at your host system's command line and hit enter.

You'll get a menu identical to the one in your mailbox from which you can read these old messages, delete them, or respond to them. It's probably a good idea to clear out your mailbox and mbox file from time to time, if only to keep them uncluttered.

Are there any drawbacks to e-mail? There are a few. One is that people seem more willing to fly off the handle electronically than in person, or over the phone. Maybe it's because it's so easy to hit r and reply to a message without pausing and reflecting a moment. That's why we have smileys (see section 2.4). There's no online equivalent yet of a return receipt: chances are your message got to where it's going, but there's no absolute way for you to know for sure unless you get a reply from the other person.

So now you're ready to send e-mail to other people on the Net. Of course, you need people's addresses to send them mail. How do you get them?

Alas, the simplest answer is not what you'd call the most elegant: you call the people up on the phone or write them a letter on paper and ask them. Residents of the electronic frontier are only beginning to develop the equivalent of phone books, and the ones that exist today are far from complete (still, later on, in chapter 6, we'll show you how to use some of these directories).

Eventually, you'll start corresponding with people, which means you'll want to know how to address mail to them. It's vital to know how to do this, because the smallest mistake—using a comma when you should have used a period, for instance—can bounce the message back to you, undelivered. In this sense, Net addresses are like phone numbers: one wrong digit and you get the wrong person. Fortunately, most Net addresses now adhere to a relatively easy-to-understand system.

Earlier, you sent yourself a mail message using just your user name. This was sort of like making a local phone call—you didn't have to dial a 1 or an area code. This also works for mail to anybody else who has an account on the same system as you.

Sending mail outside of your system, though, will require the use of the Net equivalent of area codes, called "domains." A basic Net address will look something like this:

```
tomg@world.std.com
```

Tomg is somebody's user ID, and he is at (hence the @ sign) a site (or in Internetese, a "domain") known as std.com. Large organizations often have more than one computer linked to the Internet; in this case, the name of the particular machine is world (you will quickly notice that, like boat owners, Internet computer owners always name their machines).

Domains tell you the name of the organization that runs a given e-mail site and what kind of site it is or, if it's not in the United States, what country it's located in. Large organizations may have more than one computer or gateway tied to the Internet, so you'll often see a two-part domain name; and sometimes even three- or four-part domain names.

In general, American addresses end in an organizational suffix, such as ".edu," which means the site is at a college or university. Other American suffixes include

.com for businesses,

.org for nonprofit organizations,

.gov and .mil for government and military agencies,

.net for companies or organizations that run large networks.

Sites in the rest of the world tend to use a two-letter code that represents their country. Most make sense, such as .ca for Canadian sites, but there are a couple of seemingly odd ones. Swiss sites end in .ch, while South African ones end in .za. Some U.S. sites have followed this international convention (such as well.sf.ca.us).

You'll notice that the previous addresses are all in lower case. Unlike almost everything else having anything at all to do with Unix, most Net mailing systems don't care about case, so you generally don't have to worry about capitalizing e-mail addresses. Alas, there are a few exceptions—some public-access sites do allow for capital letters in user names. When in doubt, ask the person you want to write to, or let her send you a message first (recall how a person's e-mail address is usually found on the top of her message). The domain name, the part of the address after the @ sign, never has to be capitalized.

It's all a fairly simple system that works very well, except, again, it's vital to get the address exactly right—just as you have to dial a phone number exactly right. Send a message to tomg@unm.edu (which is the University of New Mexico) when you meant to send it to tomg@umn.edu (the University of Minnesota), and your letter will either bounce back to you undelivered, or go to the wrong person.

If your message is bounced back to you as undeliverable, you'll get an ominous-looking message from MAILER-DAEMON (actually a rather benign Unix program that exists to handle mail), with an evil-looking header followed by the text of your message. Sometimes, you can tell what went wrong by looking at the first few lines of the bounced message. Besides an incorrect address, it's possible your host system does not have the other site in the "map" it maintains of other host systems. Or you could be trying to send mail to another network, such as Bitnet or CompuServe, that has special addressing requirements.

Sometimes, figuring all this out can prove highly frustrating. But remember the prime Net commandment: Ask. Send a message to your system administrator. He or she might be able to help decipher the problem.

There is one kind of address that may give your host system particular problems. There are two main ways that Unix systems exchange mail. One is known as UUCP and started out with a different addressing system than the rest of the Net. Most UUCP systems have since

switched over to the standard Net addressing system, but a few tra-
ditional sites still cling to their original type, which tends to have lots
of exclamation points in it, like this:

`uunet!somesite!othersite!mybuddy`

The problem for many host sites is that exclamation points (also
known as "bangs") now mean something special in the more common
systems or "shells" used to operate many Unix computers. This means
that addressing mail to such a site (or even responding to a message
you received from one) could confuse the poor computer to no end,
and your message might never get sent out. If that happens, try
putting backslashes in front of each exclamation point, so that you get
an address that looks like this:

`uunet\!somesite\!othersite\!mybuddy`

Note that this means you may not be able to respond to such a message
by typing a lowercase r—you may get an error message and you'll
have to create a brand-new message.

If you want to get a taste of what's possible through e-mail, start an
e-mail message to this address:

`almanac@oes.orst.edu`

Leave the "subject:" line blank. As a message, write this:

`send quote`

Or, if you're feeling a little down, write this instead:

`send moral-support`

In either case, you will get back a message within a few seconds to
a few hours (depending on the state of your host system's Internet
connection). If you simply asked for a quote, you'll get back a fortune-
cookie-like saying. If you asked for moral support, you'll also get back
a fortune-cookie-like saying, only supposedly more uplifting.

This particular "mail server" is run by Oregon State University. Its
main purpose is actually to provide a way to distribute agricultural
information via e-mail. If you'd like to find out how to use the server's
full range of services, send a message to its address with this line in
it:

`send help`

You'll quickly get back a lengthy document detailing just what's available and how to get it.

Feeling opinionated? Want to give the president of the United States a piece of your mind? Send a message to president@whitehouse.gov. Or if the vice president will do, write vice-president@whitehouse.gov.

The "mail" program is actually a very powerful one and a Net-wide standard, at least on Unix computers. But it can be hard to figure out—you can type a question mark to get a list of commands, but these may be of limited use unless you're already familiar with Unix. Fortunately, there are a couple of other mail programs that are easier to use.

2.2 Elm—A Better Way

Elm is a combination mailbox and letter-writing system that uses menus to help you navigate through mail. Most Unix-based host systems now have it online. To use it, type
elm
and hit enter. You'll get a menu of your waiting mail, along with a list of commands you can execute, that will look something like this:

```
Mailbox is '/usr/spool/mail/adamg' with 38 messages [ELM
2.3 PL11]
```

```
1 Sep 1    Christopher Davis    (13)  here's another message

2 Sep 1    Christopher Davis    (91)  This is a message from

3 Aug 31   Rita Marie Rouvali   (161) First Internet Hunt

4 Aug 31   Peter Scott/Manage   (69)  New File <UK077> Unive

5 Aug 30   Peter Scott/Manage   (64)  New File <DIR020> X.50

6 Aug 30   Peter Scott/Manage   (39)  New File <NET016> DATA

7 Aug 28   Peter Scott/Manage   (67)  Proposed Usenet group

8 Aug 28   Peter Scott/Manage   (56)  New File <DIR019> JANE

9 Aug 26   Helen Trillian Ros   (15)  Tuesday
```

```
10 Aug 26 Peter Scott/Manage  (151) Update <CWK004> Oxford
You can use any of the following commands by pressing
the first character;
d)elete or u)ndelete mail, m)ail a message, r)eply or
f)orward mail, q)uit
To read a message, press <return>. j = move down, k =
move up, ? = help
```

Each line shows the date you received the message, who sent it, how many lines long the message is, and the message's subject.

If you are using VT100 emulation, you can move up and down the menu with your up- and down-arrow keys. Otherwise, type the line number of the message you want to read or delete and hit enter.

When you read a message, it pauses every 24 lines, instead of scrolling until it's done. Hit the space bar to read the next page. You can type a lowercase r to reply or a lowercase q or i to get back to the menu (the "i" stands for "index").

At the main menu, hitting a lowercase m followed by enter will let you start a message. To delete a message, type a lowercase d. You can do this while reading the message. Or, if you are in the menu, move the cursor to the message's line and then hit d.

When you're done with elm, type a lowercase q. The program will ask if you really want to delete the messages you marked. Then, it will ask you if you want to move any messages you've read but haven't marked for deletion to a "received" file. For now, hit your n key.

Elm has a major disadvantage for the beginner. The default text editor it generally calls up when you hit your r or m key is a program called emacs. Unixoids swear by emacs, but everybody else almost always finds it impossible. Unfortunately, you can't always get away from it (or vi, another text editor often found on Unix systems), so later on we'll talk about some basic commands that will keep you from going totally nuts.

If you want to save a message to your own computer, hit s, either within the message or with your cursor on the message entry in the elm menu. A file name will pop up. f you do not like it, type a new name (you won't have to backspace). Hit enter, and the message will be saved with that file name in your "home directory" on your host system. After you exit elm, you can now download it (ask your system administrator for specifics on how to download—and upload—such files).

2.3 Pine—An Even Better Way

Pine is based on elm but includes a number of improvements that make it an ideal mail system for beginners. Like elm, pine starts you with a menu. It also has an "address book" feature that is handy for people with long or complex e-mail addresses. Hitting "A" at the main menu puts you in the address book, where you can type in the person's first name (or nickname) followed by her address. Then, when you want to send that person a message, you have to type in only her first name or nickname, and pine automatically inserts her actual address. The address book also lets you set up a mailing list. This feature allows you to send the same message to a number of people at once.

What really sets pine apart is its built-in text editor, which looks and feels a lot more like word-processing programs available for MS-DOS and Macintosh users. Not only does it have word wrap (a revolutionary concept if ever there was one), it also has a spell-checker and a search command. Best of all, all of the commands you need are listed in a two-line mini-menu at the bottom of each screen. The commands look like this:

```
^W Where is
```

The little caret is a synonym for the key marked "control" on your keyboard. To find where a particular word is in your document, you'd hit your control key and your W key at the same time, which would bring up a prompt asking you for the word to look for.

Some of pine's commands are a tad peculiar (control-V for "page down," for example), which comes from being based on a variant of emacs (which is utterly peculiar). But again, all of the commands you need are listed on that two-line mini-menu, so it shouldn't take you more than a couple of seconds to find the right one.

To use pine, type

```
pine
```

at the command line and hit enter. It's a relatively new program, so some systems may not yet have it online. But it's so easy to use, you should probably send e-mail to your system administrator urging him or her to get it!

2.4 Smileys

When you're involved in an online discussion, you can't see the smiles or shrugs that the other people might make in a live conversation to show they're only kidding. But online, there's no body language. So what you might think is funny, somebody else might take as an insult. To try to keep such misunderstandings from erupting into bitter disputes, we have smileys. Tilt your head to the left and look at the following sideways. :-). Or simply :). This is your basic "smiley." Use it to indicate people should not take that comment you just made as seriously as they might otherwise. You make a smiley by typing a colon, a hyphen, and a right parenthetical bracket. Some people prefer using the word "grin," usually in this form:

```
<grin>
```

Sometimes, though, you'll see it as *grin* or even just <g> for short. Here are some other smileys:

;-)	Wink;
:-(	Frown;
:-O	Surprise;
8-)	Wearing glasses;
=|:-)=	Abe Lincoln.

OK, so maybe the last two are a little bogus :-).

2.5 Sending E-Mail to Other Networks

There are a number of computer networks that are not directly part of the Net, but which are now connected through "gateways" that allow the passing of e-mail. Here's a list of some of the larger networks, how to send mail to them, and how their users can send mail to you:

America Online

Remove any spaces from a user's name and append "aol.com" to get this:

```
user@aol.com
```

America Online users who want to send mail to you need only put your Net address in the "to:" field before composing a message.

ATTMail

Address your message to user@attmail.com.

From ATTMail, a user would send mail to you in this form:

```
internet!domain!user
```

So if your address were nancyr@world.std.com, your correspondent would send a message to you at this address:

```
internet!world.std.com!nancyr
```

Bitnet

Users of Bitnet (and NetNorth in Canada and EARN in Europe) often have addresses in this form: IZZY@INDVMS. If you're lucky, all you'll have to do to mail to that address is add "bitnet" at the end, to get izzy@indvms.bitnet. Sometimes, however, mail to such an address will bounce back to you, because Bitnet addresses do not always translate well into an Internet form. If this happens, you can send mail through one of two Internet/Bitnet gateways. First, change the @ in the address to a %, so that you get username%site.bitnet. Then add either @vm.marist.edu or @cunyvm.cuny.edu, so that, with the previous example, you would get izzy%indyvms.bitnet@vm.marist.edu or izzy%indvyvms.bitnet@cunyvm.cuny.edu

Bitnet users have it a little easier: they can usually send mail directly to your e-mail address without fooling around with it at all. So send them your address and they should be OK.

CompuServe

CompuServe users have numerical addresses in this form: 73727,545. To send mail to a CompuServe user, change the comma to a period and add "@compuserve.com"; for example:

```
73727.545@compuserve.com.
```

Note that some CompuServe users must pay extra to receive mail from the Internet.

If you know CompuServe users who want to send you mail, tell them to GO MAIL and create a mail message. In the address area, instead of typing in a CompuServe number, have them type your address in this form:

```
>INTERNET:YourID@YourAddress.
```

For example, >INTERNET:adamg@world.std.com. Note that both the ">" and the ":" are required.

Delphi

To send mail to a Delphi user, the form is username@delphi.com.

Fidonet

To send mail to people using a Fidonet BBS, you need the name they use to log onto that system and its "node number." Fidonet node numbers or addresses consist of three numbers, in this form: 1:322/190. The first number tells which of several broad geographic zones the BBS is in (1 represents the United States and Canada, 2 Europe and Israel, 3 Pacific Asia, 4 South America). The second number represents the BBS's network, while the final number is the BBS's "FidoNode" number in that network. If your correspondent gives you only two numbers (for example, 322/190), it means the system is in zone 1.

Now comes the tricky part. You have to reverse the numbers and add to them the letters f, n, and z (which stand for "FidoNode," "network," and "zone"). For example, the previous address would become

```
f190.n322.z1.
```

Now add "fidonet.org" at the end, to get f190.n322.z1.fidonet.org. Then add "FirstName.LastName@," to get this:

```
FirstName.LastName@f190.n322.z1.fidonet.org
```

Note the period between the first and last names. Also, some countries now have their own Fidonet "backbone" systems, which might affect addressing. For example, were the address in Germany, you would end it with "fido.de" instead of "fidonet.org."

Whew!

The reverse process is totally different. First, the person has to have access to his or her BBS's "net mail" area and know the Fidonet address of his or her local Fidonet/UUCP gateway (often the system operator, or "sysop," will know it). Your Fidonet correspondents should address a net-mail message to UUCP (not your name) in the "to:" field. In the node-number field, they should type in the node number of the Fidonet/UUCP gateway (if the gateway system is in the same regional network as their system, they need only type the last number, for example, 390 instead of 322/390). Then, the first line of the message has to be your Internet address, followed by a blank line. After that, they can write the message and send it.

Because of the way Fidonet moves mail, it could take a day or two for a message to be delivered in either direction. Also, because many Fidonet systems are run as hobbies, it is considered good form to ask the gateway sysop's permission if you intend to pass large amounts of mail back and forth. Messages of a commercial nature are strictly forbidden (even if it's something the other person asked for). Also, consider it very likely that somebody other than the recipient will read your messages.

GEnie

To send mail to a GEnie user, add "@genie.geis.com" to the end of the GEnie user name, for example: walt@genie.geis.com.

MCIMail

To send mail to somebody with an MCIMail account, add "@mci-mail.com" to the end of the name or numerical address. For example:

```
555-1212@mcimail.com
```

or

```
jsmith@mcimail.com
```

Note that if there is more than one MCIMail subscriber with that name, you will get a mail message back from MCI giving you their names and numerical addresses. You'll then have to figure out which one you want and resend the message.

From MCI, a user would type

```
Your Name (EMS)
```

at the "To:" prompt. At the EMS prompt, the user would type

```
internet
```

followed by your Net address at the "Mbx:" prompt.

Peacenet

To send mail to a Peacenet user, use this form:

```
username@igc.org
```

Peacenet subscribers can use your regular address to send you mail.

Prodigy

UserID@prodigy.com. Note that Prodigy users must pay extra for Internet e-mail.

2.6 Seven Unix Commands You Can't Live Without

If you connect to the Net through a Unix system, eventually you'll have to come to terms with Unix. For better or worse, most Unix systems do NOT shield you from their inner workings—if you want to copy a Usenet posting to a file, for example, you'll have to use some Unix commands if you ever want to do anything with that file.

Like MS-DOS, Unix is an operating system—it tells the computer how to do things. Now although Unix may have a reputation as being even more complex than MS-DOS, in most cases a few basic, and simple, commands should be all you'll ever need.

If your own computer uses MS-DOS or PC-DOS, the basic concepts will seem very familiar—but watch out for the cd command, which works differently enough from the similarly named DOS command that it will drive you crazy. Also, unlike MS-DOS, Unix is case sensitive—if you type commands or directory names in the wrong case, you'll get an error message.

If you're used to working on a Mac, you'll have to remember that Unix stores files in "directories" rather than "folders." Unix directories are organized like branches on a tree. At the bottom is the "root" directory, with subdirectories branching off that (and subdirectories in turn can have subdirectories). The Mac equivalent of a Unix subdirectory is a folder within another folder.

cat   Equivalent to the MS-DOS "type" command. To pause a file every screen, type

```
cat file |more
```

where "file" is the name of the file you want to see. Hitting control-C will stop the display. Alternately, you could type

```
more file
```

to achieve the same result. You can also use cat for writing or uploading text files to your name or home directory (similar to the MS-DOS "copy con" command). If you type

```
cat>test
```

you start a file called "test." You can either write something simple (no editing once you've finished a line, and you have to hit return at the end of each line) or upload something into that file using your communications software's ASCII protocol). To close the file, hit control-D.

cd   The "change directory" command. To change from your present directory to another, type

```
cd directory
```

and hit enter. Unlike MS-DOS, which uses a \ to denote subdirectories (for example: \stuff\text), Unix uses a / (for example: /stuff/text). So to change from your present directory to the stuff/text subdirectory, you would type

```
cd stuff/text
```

and then hit enter. As in MS-DOS, you do not need the first backslash if the subdirectory comes off the directory you're already in. To move back up a directory tree, you would type

```
cd ..
```

followed by enter. Note the space between the cd and the two periods—this is where MS-DOS users will really go nuts.

cp   Copies a file. The syntax is

```
cp file1 file2
```

which would copy file1 to file2 (or overwrite file2 with file1).

ls   This command, when followed by enter, tells you what's in the directory, similar to the DOS dir command, except in alphabetical order.

```
ls  |more
```

will stop the listing every 24 lines—handy if there are a lot of things in the directory. The basic ls command does not list "hidden" files, such as the .login file that controls how your system interacts with Unix. To see these files, type

```
ls -a
```

or

```
ls -a |more
```

ls -l will tell you the size of each file in bytes and when each was created or modified.

mv   Similar to the MS-DOS rename command.

```
mv file1 file2
```

will rename file1 as file2, The command can also be used to move files between directories.

```
mv file1 News
```

would move file1 to your News directory.

rm   Deletes a file. Type

```
rm filename
```

and hit enter (but beware: when you hit enter, it's gone for good).

Wildcards

When searching for, copying, or deleting files, you can use "wildcards" if you are not sure of the file's exact name.

```
ls man*
```

would find the following files:

```
manual, manual.txt, man-o-man.
```

Use a question mark when you're sure about all but one or two characters. For example,

```
ls man?
```

would find a file called mane, but not one called manual.

2.7 When Things Go Wrong

• You send a message but get back an ominous looking message from MAILER-DAEMON containing up to several dozen lines of computerese followed by your message.

Somewhere in those lines you can often find a clue to what went wrong. You might have made a mistake in spelling the e-mail address. The site to which you're sending mail might have been down for maintenance or a problem. You may have used the wrong "translation" for mail to a non-Internet network.

• You call up your host system's text editor to write a message or reply to one and can't seem to get out.

If it's emacs, try control-X, control-C (in other words, hit your control key and your X key at the same time, followed by control and C). If worse comes to worst, you can hang up.

• In elm, you accidentally hit the D key for a message you want to save.

Type the number of the message, hit enter, and then U, which will "undelete" the message. This works only before you exit elm; once you quit, the message is gone.

• You try to upload an ASCII message you've written on your own computer into a message you're preparing in elm or pine and you get a lot of left brackets; capital Ms, Ks, and Ls; and some funny-looking characters.

Believe it or not, your message will actually wind up looking fine; all that garbage is temporary and reflects the problems some Unix text processors have with ASCII uploads. But it will take much longer for your upload to finish. One way to deal with this is to call up the simple mail program, which will not produce any weird characters when you upload a text file into a message. Another way (which is better if your prepared message is a response to somebody's mail) is to create a text file on your host system with cat, for example,

```
cat>file
```

and then upload your text into that. Then, in elm or pine, you can insert the message with a simple command (control-R in pine, for example); only this time you won't see all that extraneous stuff.

3 Usenet I

3.1 The Global Watering Hole

Imagine a conversation carried out over a period of hours and days, as if people were leaving messages and responses on a bulletin board. Or imagine the electronic equivalent of a radio talk show where everybody can put their two cents in and no one is ever on hold.

Unlike e-mail, which is usually "one-to-one," Usenet is "many-to-many." Usenet is the international meeting place, where people gather to meet their friends, discuss the day's events, keep up with computer trends, or talk about whatever's on their mind. Jumping into a Usenet discussion can be a liberating experience. Nobody knows what you look or sound like, how old you are, what your background is. You're judged solely on your words, your ability to make a point.

To many people, Usenet IS the Net. In fact, it is often confused with Internet. But it is a totally separate system. All Internet sites CAN carry Usenet, but so do many non-Internet sites, from sophisticated Unix machines to old XT clones and Apple IIs.

Technically, Usenet messages are shipped around the world, from host system to host system, using one of several specific Net protocols. Your host system stores all of its Usenet messages in one place, which everybody with an account on the system can access. That way, no matter how many people actually read a given message, each host system has to store only one copy of it. Many host systems "talk" with several others regularly in case one or another of their links goes down for some reason. When two host systems connect, they basically compare notes on which Usenet messages they already have. Any that one is missing, the other then transmits, and vice versa. Because they are computers, they don't mind running through thousands, even millions, of these comparisons every day.

Yes, millions. For Usenet is huge. Every day, Usenet users pump upward of 40 million characters a day into the system—roughly the equivalent of volumes A–G of the *Encyclopedia Britannica*. Obviously, nobody could possibly keep up with this immense flow of messages. Let's look at how to find conferences and discussions of interest to you.

The basic building block of Usenet is the newsgroup, which is a collection of messages with a related theme (on other networks, these would be called conferences, forums, bboards, or special-interest groups). There are now more than five thousand of these newsgroups, in several different languages, covering everything from art to zoology, from science fiction to South Africa.

Some public-access systems, typically the ones that work through menus, try to make it easier by dividing Usenet into several broad categories. Choose one of those and you're given a list of newsgroups in that category. Then select the newsgroup you're interested in and start reading.

Other systems let you compile your own "reading list" so that you only see messages in conferences you want. In both cases, conferences are arranged in a particular hierarchy devised in the early 1980s. Newsgroup names start with one of a series of broad topic names. For example, newsgroups beginning with "comp." are about particular computer-related topics. These broad topics are followed by a series of more focused topics (so that "comp.unix" groups are limited to discussion about Unix). Here are the main hierarchies:

bionet	Research biology
bit.listserv	Conferences originating as Bitnet mailing lists
biz	Business
comp	Computers and related subjects
misc	Discussions that don't fit anywhere else
news	News about Usenet itself
rec	Hobbies
sci	Science other than research biology
soc	"Social" groups
talk	Politics and related topics
alt	Controversial or unusual topics; not carried by all sites

In addition, many host systems carry newsgroups for a particular city, state, or region. For example, ne.housing is a newsgroup where New Englanders look for apartments. A growing number also carry K12 newsgroups, which are aimed at elementary and secondary teachers and students. And a number of sites carry clari newsgroups, which is actually a commercial service consisting of wire-service stories and a unique online computer news service (more on this in chapter 10). .

3.2 Navigating Usenet with nn

How do you dive right in? As mentioned, on some systems, it's all done through menus—you just keep choosing from a list of choices until you get to the newsgroup you want and then hit the "read" command. On Unix systems, however, you will have to use a "newsreader" program. Two of the more common ones are known as rn (for "read news") and nn (for "no news"—because it's supposed to be simpler to use).

For beginners, nn may be the better choice because it works with menus—you get a list of articles in a given newsgroup and then you choose which ones you want to see. To try it out, connect to your host system and, at the command line, type

```
nn news.announce.newusers
```

and hit enter. After a few seconds, you should see something like this:

```
Newsgroup: news.announce.newusers  Articles: 22 of 22/1
NEW

a  Gene Spafford   776 Answers to Frequently Asked Ques

b  Gene Spafford   362 A Primer on How to Work With th

c  Gene Spafford   387 Emily Postnews Answers Your Ques

d  Gene Spafford   101 Hints on writing style for Usene

e  Gene Spafford   74  Introduction to news.announce

f  Gene Spafford   367 USENET Software: History and Sou

g  Gene Spafford   353 What is Usenet?

h  taylor          241 A Guide to Social Newsgroups and
```

```
i   Gene Spafford   585 Alternative Newsgroup Hierarchies

j   Gene Spafford   455 >Alternative Newsgroup Hierarchie

k   David C Lawrenc151 How to Create a New Newsgroup

l   Gene Spafford   106 How to Get Information about Net

m   Gene Spafford   888 List of Active Newsgroups

n   Gene Spafford   504 List of Moderators

o   Gene Spafford   1051 Publicly Accessible Mailing List

p   Gene Spafford   1123 Publicly Accessible Mailing List

q   Gene Spafford   1193 >Publicly Accessible Mailing Lis

r   Jonathan Kamens 644 How to become a USENET site

s   Jonathan Kamen  1344 List of Periodic Informational P

--15:52-SELECT-help:?-----Top 85%-----

Explanatory postings for new users. (Moderated)
```

Obviously, this is a good newsgroup to begin your exploration of Usenet! Here's what all this means: The first letter on each line is the letter you type to read that particular "article" (it makes sense that a "newsgroup" would have "articles"). Next comes the name of the person who wrote that article, followed by its length, in lines, and what the article is about. At the bottom, you see the local time at your access site, what you're doing right now (SELECTing articles), which key to hit for some help (the ? key), and how many of the articles in the newsgroup you can see on this screen. The "(Moderated)" means the newsgroup has a "moderator" who is the only one who can directly post messages to it. This is generally limited to groups such as this, which contain articles of basic information, or for digests, which are basically online magazines (more on them in a bit).

Say you're particularly interested in what "Emily Postnews" has to say about proper etiquette on Usenet. Hit your c key (lower case!), and the line will light up. If you want to read something else, hit the key that corresponds to it. And if you want to see what's on the next page of articles, hit return or your space bar.

But you're impatient to get going, and you want to read that article now. The command for that in nn is a capital Z. Hit it and you'll see something like this:

```
Gene Spafford: Emily Postnews Answers Your Questions on
NetiquetteSep 92 04:17 Original-author: brad@look-
ing.on.ca (Brad Templeton)
Archive-name: emily-postnews/part1
Last-change: 30 Nov 91 by brad@looking.on.ca (Brad Tem-
pleton)

**NOTE: this is intended to be satirical. If you do not
recognize it as such, consult a doctor or professional
comedian. The recommendations in this article should rec-
ognized for what they are—admonitions about what NOT to
do.

               "Dear Emily Postnews"

   Emily Postnews, foremost authority on proper net
                   behaviour,
     gives her advice on how to act on the net.


================================================================

Dear Miss Postnews: How long should my signature be?—ver-
bose@noisy

A: Dear Verbose: Please try and make your signature as
long as you--09:57--.announce.newusers--LAST--help:?
  --Top 4%--
```

The first few lines are the message's header, similar to the header you get in e-mail messages. Then comes the beginning of the message. The last line tells you the time again, the newsgroup name (or part of it, anyway), the position in your message stack that this message occupies, how to get help, and how much of the message is on screen. If you want to keep reading this message, just hit your space bar (not your enter key!) for the next screen and so on until done. When done, you'll be returned to the newsgroup menu. For now hit Q (upper case this time), which quits you out of nn and returns you to your host system's command line.

To get a look at another interesting newsgroup, type

```
nn comp.risks
```

and hit enter. This newsgroup is another moderated group, this time a digest of all the funny and frightening ways computers and the people who run and use them can go wrong. Again, you read articles by selecting their letters. If you're in the middle of an article and decide you want to go onto the next one, hit your n key.

Now it's time to look for some newsgroups that might be of particular interest to you. Unix host systems that have nn use a program called nngrep (ever get the feeling Unix was not entirely written in English?) that lets you scan newsgroups. Exit nn and at your host system's command line, type

```
nngrep word
```

where word is the subject you're interested in. If you use a Macintosh computer, you might try

```
nngrep mac
```

You'll get something that looks like this:

```
alt.music.machines.of.loving.grace
alt.religion.emacs
comp.binaries.mac
comp.emacs
comp.lang.forth.mac
comp.os.mach
comp.sources.mac
comp.sys.mac.announce
comp.sys.mac.apps
comp.sys.mac.comm
comp.sys.mac.databases
comp.sys.mac.digest
comp.sys.mac.games
comp.sys.mac.hardware
comp.sys.mac.hypercard
comp.sys.mac.misc
comp.sys.mac.programmer
comp.sys.mac.system
comp.sys.mac.wanted
gnu.emacs.announce
gnu.emacs.bug
```

```
gnu.emacs.gnews
gnu.emacs.gnus
gnu.emacs.help
gnu.emacs.lisp.manual
gnu.emacs.sources
gnu.emacs.vm.bug
gnu.emacs.vm.info
gnu.emacs.vms
```

Note that some of these obviously have something to do with Macintoshes while some obviously do not; nngrep is not a perfect system. If you want to get a list of ALL the newsgroups available on your host system, type

```
nngrep -a |more
```

or

```
nngrep -a |pg
```

and hit enter (which one to use depends on the Unix used on your host system; if one doesn't do anything, try the other). You don't absolutely need the |more or |pg, but if you don't include it, the list will keep scrolling, rather than pausing every 24 lines. If you are in nn, hitting a capital Y will bring up a similar list.

Typing "nn newsgroup" for every newsgroup can get awfully tiring after a while. When you use nn, your host system looks in a file called .newsrc. This is basically a list of every newsgroup on the host system along with notations on which groups and articles you have read (all maintained by the computer). You can also use this file to create a "reading list" that brings up each newsgroup to which you want to "subscribe." To try it out, type

```
nn
```

without any newsgroup name, and hit enter.

Unfortunately, you will start out with a .newsrc file that has you "subscribed" to every single newsgroup on your host system! To delete a newsgroup from your reading list, type a capital U while its menu is on the screen. The computer will ask you if you're sure you want to "unsubscribe." If you then hit a Y, you'll be unsubscribed and put in the next group.

With many host systems carrying thousands of newsgroups, this will take you forever. Fortunately, there are a couple of easier ways to do this. Both involve calling up your .newsrc file in a word or text processor. In a .newsrc file, each newsgroup takes up one line, consisting of the group's name, an exclamation point or a colon, and a range of numbers. Newsgroups with a colon are ones to which you are subscribed; those followed by an exclamation point are "unsubscribed." To start with a clean slate, then, you have to change all those colons to exclamation points.

If you know how to use emacs or vi, call up the .newsrc file (you might want to make a copy of .newsrc first, just in case), and use the search-and-replace function to make the change.

If you're not comfortable with these text processors, you can download the .newsrc file, make the changes on your own computer, and then upload the revised file. Before you download the file, however, you should do a couple of things. One is to type

```
cp .newsrc temprc
```

and hit enter. You will actually download this temprc file (note the name does not start with a period—some computers, such as those using MS-DOS, do not allow file names starting with periods). After you download the file, open it in your favorite word processor and use its search-and-replace function to change the exclamation points to colons. Be careful not to change anything else! Save the document in ASCII or text format. Dial back into your host system. At the command line, type

```
cp temprc temprc1
```

and hit enter. This new file will serve as your backup .newsrc file just in case something goes wrong. Upload the temprc file from your computer. This will overwrite the Unix system's old temprc file. Now type

```
cp temprc .newsrc
```

and hit enter. You now have a clean slate to start creating a reading list.

3.3 nn Commands

To mark a specific article for reading, type the letter next to it (in lower case). To mark a specific article and all of its responses, type the letter and an asterisk, for example:

a*

To unselect an article, type the letter next to it (again, in lower case).

C   Cancels an article (around the world) that you
                        wrote. Every article posted on Usenet has a unique
                        ID number. Hitting a capital C sends out a new
                        message that tells host systems that receive it to
                        find the earlier message and delete it.

F   To post a public response, or followup. If selected
                        while still on a newsgroup "page," asks you which
                        article to follow up. If selected while in a specific
                        page, will follow up that article. In either case,
                        you'll be asked if you want to include the original
                        article in yours. Caution: puts you in whatever text
                        editor is your default.

N   Goes to the next subscribed newsgroup with
                        unread articles.

P   Goes to the previous subscribed newsgroup with
                        unread articles.

G news.group   Goes to a specific newsgroup. Can be used to
                        subscribe to new newsgroups. Hitting G brings up
                        a submenu:

                        u   Goes to the group and shows only unread
                             articles.

                        a   Goes to the group and shows all articles.

                        s   Will show you only articles with a specific
                             subject.

                        n   Will show you only articles from a specific
                             person.

M   Mails a copy of the current article to somebody.
                        You'll be asked for the recipient's e-mail address
                        and whether you want to add any comments to the
                        article before sending it off. As with F, puts you in
                        the default editor.

:post   Post an article. You'll be asked for the name of the
                        group.

Q   Quit, exit, nn.

U	Unsubscribe from the current newsgroup.
R	Responds to an article via e-mail.
space	Hitting the space bar brings up the next page of articles.
X	If you have selected articles, it marks all articles as read and takes you to the next unread subscribed newsgroup.
=word	Finds and marks all articles in the newsgroup with a specific word in the "subject:" line, for example:
	`=modem`
Z	Shows you selected articles immediately and then returns you to the current newsgroup.
?	Brings up a help screen.
<	Goes to the previous page in the newsgroup.
>	Goes to the next page in the newsgroup.
$	Goes to the last page in an article.
^	Goes to the first page in an article.

3.4 Using rn

Some folks prefer this older newsreader.

If you type

```
rn news.announce.newusers
```

at your host system's command line, you'll see something like this:

```
******** 21 unread articles in news.announce.newusers--
read now? [ynq]
```

If you hit your Y key, the first article will appear on your screen. If you want to see what articles are available first, though, hit your computer's = key and you'll get something like this:

```
152 Introduction to news.announce
153 A Primer on How to Work With the Usenet Community
154 What is Usenet?
155 Answers to Frequently Asked Questions
156 Hints on writing style for Usenet
```

End of article 158 (of 178)—what next? [npq]

Notice how the messages are in numerical order this time, and don't tell you who sent them. Article 154 looks interesting. To read it, type in 154 and hit enter. You'll see something like this:

```
Article 154 (20 more) in news.announce.newusers
  (moderated):
From: spaf@cs.purdue.EDU (Gene Spafford)
Newsgroups: news.announce.newusers,news.admin,news.an-
swers
Subject: What is Usenet?
Date: 20 Sep 92 04:17:26 GMT
Followup-To: news.newusers.questions
Organization: Dept. of Computer Sciences, Purdue Univ.
Lines: 353
Supersedes: <spaf-whatis_715578719@cs.purdue.edu>
Archive-name: what-is-usenet/part1
Original from: chip@tct.com (Chip Salzenberg)
Last-change: 19 July 1992 by spaf@cs.purdue.edu (Gene
Spafford)

The first thing to understand about Usenet is that it is
widely misunderstood. Every day on Usenet, the "blind
men and the elephant" phenomenon is evident, in spades.
```

In my opinion, more flame wars arise because of a lack
of understanding of the nature of Usenet than from any
other source. And consider that such flame wars arise,
of necessity, among people who are on Usenet. Imagine,
then, how poorly understood Usenet must be by those outside!

--MORE--(7%)

This time, the header looks much more like the gobbledygook you
get in e-mail messages. To keep reading, hit your space bar. If you hit
your n key (lower case), you'll go to the next message in the numerical
order.

To escape rn, just keep hitting your q key (in lower case), until you
get back to the command line. Now let's set up your reading list.
Because rn uses the same .newsrc file as nn, you can use one of the
search-and-replace methods described previously. Or you can do this:
Type

rn

and hit enter. When the first newsgroup comes up on your screen, hit
your u key (in lower case). Hit it again, and again, and again. Or just
keep it pressed down (if your computer starts beeping, let up for a
couple of seconds). Eventually, you'll be told you're at the end of the
newsgroups, and asked what you want to do next.

Here's where you begin entering newsgroups. Type

g newsgroup

(for example, g comp.sys.mac.announce) and hit enter. You'll be asked
if you want to "subscribe." Hit your y key. Then type

g next newsgroup

(for example, g comp.announce.newusers) and hit enter. Repeat until
done. This process will also set up your reading list for nn, if you
prefer that newsreader. But how do you know which newsgroups to
subscribe to? Typing a lowercase l and then hitting enter will show
you a list of all available newsgroups. Again, since there could be more
than two thousand newsgroups on your system, this might not be
something you want to do. Fortunately, you can search for groups with
particular words in their names, using the l command. Typing

```
l mac
```

followed by enter will bring up a list of newsgroups with those letters in them (and as in nn, you will also see groups dealing with emacs and the like, in addition to groups related to Macintosh computers).

Because of the vast amount of messages transmitted over Usenet, most systems carry messages for only a few days or weeks. So if there's a message you want to keep, you should either turn on your computer's screen capture or save it to a file that you can later download. To save a message as a file in rn, type

```
s filename
```

where filename is what you want to call the file. Hit enter. You'll be asked if you want to save it in "mailbox format." In most cases, you can answer with an n (which will strip off the header). The message will now be saved to a file in your News directory (which you can access by typing cd News and then hitting enter).

Also, some newsgroups fill up particularly quickly—go away for a couple of days and you'll come back to find hundreds of articles! One way to deal with that is to mark them as "read" so that they no longer appear on your screen. In nn, hit a capital J; in rn, a small c.

3.5 rn Commands

Different commands are available to you in rn depending on whether you are already in a newsgroup or reading a specific article. At any point, typing a lowercase h will bring up a list of available commands and some terse instructions for using them. Here are some of them:

After you've just called up rn, or within a newsgroup:

c   Marks every article in a newsgroup as read (or "caught up") so that you don't have to see them again. The system will ask you if you are sure. Can be done either when asked if you want to read a particular newsgroup or once in the newsgroup.

           ```
           g news.group
           ```

           Use this both for going to groups to which you're already subscribed and subscribing to new groups.

h   Provides a list of available commands with terse instructions.

l   Gives a list of all available newsgroups.

p   Goes to the first previous subscribed newsgroup with unread articles.

q   Quits

Only within a newsgroup:

=   Gives a list of all available articles in the newsgroup.

m   Marks a specific article or series of articles as "unread" again so that you can come back to them later. Typing

```
1700m
```

and hitting enter would mark just that article as unread. Typing

```
1700-1800m
```

and hitting enter would mark all of those articles as unread.

space   Brings up the next page of article listings. If already on the last page, displays the first article in the newsgroup.

u   Unsubscribes you from the newsgroup.

/text/   Searches through the newsgroup for articles with a specific word or phrase in the "subject:" line, from the current article to the end of the newsgroup. For example,

```
/EFF/
```

would bring you to the first article with "EFF" in the "subject:" line.

?text?   The same as /text/ except it searches in reverse order from the current article.

Only within a specific article:

e   Some newsgroups consist of articles that are binary files, typically programs or graphics images. Hitting e will convert the ASCII characters within such an article into a file you can then download and use or view (assuming you have the proper computer and software). Many times, such files will be split into several articles; just keep calling up the articles and hitting e until done. You'll find the resulting file in your News subdirectory.

C	If you post an article and then decide it was a mistake, call it up on your host system and hit this. The message will soon begin disappearing from systems around the world.
F	Posts a public response in the newsgroup to the current article. Includes a copy of the original posting, which you can then edit down using your host system's text editor.
f	The same as uppercase F except it does not include a copy of the original message in yours.
m	Marks the current article as "unread" so that you can come back to it later. You do not have to type the article number.
Control-N	Brings up the first response to the article. If there is no follow-up article, this returns you to the first unread article in the newsgroup.
Control-P	Goes to the message to which the current article is a reply.
n	Goes to the next unread article in the newsgroup.
N	Takes you to the next article in the newsgroup even if you've already read it.
q	Quits, or exits, the current article. Leaves you in the current newsgroup.
R	Replies, via e-mail only, to the author of the current article. Includes a copy of the original message in yours.
r	The same as uppercase R, except it does not include a copy of the original article.
s file	Copies the current article to a file in your News directory, where "file" is the name of the file you want to save it to. You'll be asked if you want to use "mailbox" format when saving. If you answer by hitting your N key, most of the header will not be saved.
s l mail user	Mails a copy of the article to somebody. For "user" substitute an e-mail address. Does not let you add comments to the message first, however.

space   Hitting the space bar shows the next page of the article, or, if at the end, goes to the next unread article.

3.6 Essential Newsgroups

With so much to choose from, everybody will likely have their own unique Usenet reading list. But there are a few newsgroups that are particularly of interest to newcomers. Among them:

news.announce.newusers   This group consists of a series of articles that explain various facets of Usenet.

news.newusers.questions   This is where you can ask questions (we'll see how in a bit) about how Usenet works.

news.announce.newsgroups   Look here for information about new or proposed newsgroups.

news.answers   Contains lists of "Frequently Asked Questions" (FAQs) and their answers from many different newsgroups. Learn how to fight jet lag in the FAQ from rec.travel.air, look up answers to common questions about Microsoft Windows in an FAQ from comp.os.ms-windows, etc.

alt.internet.services   Looking for something in particular on the Internet? Ask here.

alt.infosystems.announce   People adding new information services to the Internet will post details here.

3.7 Speaking Up

"Threads" are an integral part of Usenet. When somebody posts a message, often somebody else will respond. Soon, a thread of conversation begins. Following these threads is relatively easy. In nn, related messages are grouped together. In rn, when you're done with a message, you can hit control-N to read the next related message, or followup. As you explore Usenet, it's probably a good idea to read discussions for a while before you jump in. This way, you can get a feel for the particular newsgroup—each has its own rhythms.

Eventually, though, you'll want to speak up. There are two main ways to do this. You can join an existing conversation, or you can start a whole new thread.

If you want to join a discussion, you have to decide if you want to include portions of the message you are responding to in your message. The reason to do this is so people can see what you're responding to, just in case the original message has disappeared from their system (remember that most Usenet messages have a short life span on the average host system) or they can't find it.

If you're using a Unix host system, joining an existing conversation is similar in both nn and rn: hit your F key when done with a given article in the thread. In rn, type a small f if you don't want to include portions of the message you're responding to; an uppercase F if you do. In nn, type a capital F. You'll then be asked if you want to include portions of the original message.

And here's where you hit another Unix wall. When you hit your F key, your host system calls up its basic Unix text editor. If you're lucky, that'll be Pico, a very easy system. More likely, however, you'll get dumped into emacs (or possibly vi), which you've already met in the chapter on e-mail.

The single most important emacs command is this one:

```
control-x control-c
```

This means, depress your control key and hit x. Then depress the control key and hit c. Memorize this. In fact, it's so important, it bears repeating:

```
control-x control-c
```

These keystrokes are how you get out of emacs. If they work well, you'll be asked if you want to send, edit, abort, or list the message you were working on. If they don't work well (say you accidentally hit some other weird key combination that means something special to emacs) and nothing seems to happen, or you just get more weird-looking emacs prompts on the bottom of your screen, try hitting control-G. This should stop whatever emacs was trying to do (you should see the word "quit" on the bottom of your screen), after which you can hit control-X control-C. But if this still doesn't work, remember that you can always disconnect and dial back in!

If you have told your newsreader you do want to include portions of the original message in yours, it will automatically put the entire thing at the top of your message. Use the arrow keys to move down to the lines you want to delete and hit control-K, which will delete one line at a time.

You can then write your message. Remember that you have to hit enter before your cursor gets to the end of the line, because emacs does not have word wrapping.

When done, hit control-X control-C. You'll be asked the question about sending, editing, aborting, etc. Chose one. If you hit Y, your host system will start the process to sending your message across the Net.

The nn and rn programs work differently when it comes to posting entirely new messages. In nn, type

```
:post
```

and hit enter in any newsgroup. You'll be asked which newsgroup to post a message to. Type in its name and hit enter. Then you'll be asked for "keywords." These are words you'd use to attract somebody scanning a newsgroup. Say you're selling your car. You might type the type of car here. Next comes a "summary" line, which is somewhat similar. Finally, you'll be asked for the message's "distribution." This is where you put how widely you want your message disseminated. Think about this one for a second. If you are selling your car, it makes little sense to send a message about it all over the world. But if you want to talk about the environment, it might make a lot of sense. Each host system has its own set of distribution classifications, but there's generally a local one (just for users of that system); one for the city, state, or region it's in; another for the country (for example, usa); one for the continent (for Americans and Canadians, na); and finally, one for the entire world (usually, world).

Which one to use? Generally, a couple of seconds' thought will help you decide. If you're selling your car, use your city or regional distribution—people in Australia won't much care and may even get annoyed. If you want to discuss presidential politics, using a USA distribution makes more sense. If you want to talk about events in the Middle East, sending your message to the entire world is perfectly acceptable.

Then you can type your message. If you've composed your message offline (generally a good idea if you and emacs don't get along), you can upload it now. You may see a lot of weird-looking characters as it uploads into emacs, but those will disappear when you hit control-X and then control-C. Alternately, "save" the message (for example, by hitting m in rn), log out, compose your message offline, log back on, and upload your message into a file on your host system. Then call up Usenet and find the article you "saved." Start a reply, and you'll be asked if you want to include a prepared message. Type in the name of the file you just created and hit enter.

In rn, you have to wait until you get to the end of a newsgroup to hit F, which will bring up a message-composing system. Alternately, at your host system's command line, you can type

```
Pnews
```

and hit enter. You'll be prompted somewhat similarly to the nn system, except that you'll be given a list of possible distributions. If you chose "world," you'll get this message:

```
This program posts news to thousands of machines through-
out the entire civilized world. Your message will cost
the net hundreds if not thousands of dollars to send
everywhere. Please be sure you know what you are doing.

Are you absolutely sure that you want to do this? [ny]
```

Don't worry—your message won't really cost the Net untold amounts, although, again, it's a good idea to think for a second whether your message really should go everywhere.

If you want to respond to a given post through e-mail, instead of publicly, hit R in nn or r or R in rn. In rn, as with follow-up articles, the upper-case key includes the original message in yours.

Most newsgroups are unmoderated, which means that every message you post will eventually wind up on every host system within the geographic region you specified that carries that newsgroup.

Some newsgroups, however, are moderated, as you saw earlier with comp.risks. In these groups, messages are shipped to a single location where a moderator, acting much like a magazine editor, decides what actually gets posted. In some cases, groups are moderated like scholarly journals. In other cases, it's to try to cut down on the massive number of messages that might otherwise be posted.

You'll notice that many articles in Usenet end with a fancy "signature" that often contains some witty saying, a clever drawing, and, almost incidentally, the poster's name and e-mail address. You too can have your own "signature" automatically appended to everything you post. On your own computer, create a signature file. Try to keep it to four lines or less, lest you annoy others on the Net. Then, while connected to your host system, type

```
cat>.signature
```

and hit enter (note the period before the s). Upload your signature file into this using your communications software's ASCII upload protocol. When done, hit control-D, the Unix command for closing a file. Now, every time you post a message, this will be appended to it.

There are a few caveats to posting. Usenet is no different from a Town Meeting or publication: you're not supposed to break the law, whether that's posting copyrighted material or engaging in illegal activities. It is also not a place to try to sell products (except in certain biz. and for-sale newsgroups).

3.8 Cross-Posting

Sometimes, you'll have an issue you think should be discussed in more than one Usenet newsgroup. Rather than posting individual messages in each group, you can post the same message in several groups at once, through a process known as cross-posting.

Say you want to start a discussion about the political ramifications of importing rare tropical fish from Brazil. People who read rec.aquaria might have something to say. So might people who read alt.politics.animals and talk.politics.misc.

Cross-posting is easy. It also should mean that people on other systems who subscribe to several newsgroups will see your message only once, rather than several times—news-reading software can cancel out the other copies once a person has read the message. When you get ready to post a message (whether through Pnews for rn or the :post command in nn), you'll be asked in which newsgroups. Type the names of the various groups, separated by a comma, but no space, for example

```
rec.aquaria,alt.politics.animals,talk.politics.misc
```

and hit enter. After you answer the other questions (geographic distribution, etc.), the message will be posted in the various groups (unless one of the groups is moderated, in which case the message goes to the moderator, who decides whether to make it public).

It's considered bad form to post to an excessive number of newsgroups, or inappropriate newsgroups. Chances are, you don't really
have to post something in 20 different places. And while you may
think your particular political issue is vitally important to the fate of
the world, probably the readers of rec.arts.comics will not, or at least
not important enough to impose on them. You'll get a lot of nasty
e-mail messages demanding you restrict your messages to the "appropriate" newsgroups.

4 Usenet II

4.1 Flame, Blather, and Spew

Something about online communications seems to make some people particularly irritable. Perhaps it's the immediacy and semi-anonymity of it all. Whatever it is, there are whole classes of people you will soon think seem to exist to make you miserable.

Rather than pausing and reflecting on a message as one might do with a letter received on paper, it's just so easy to hit your R key and tell people you don't really know what you really think of them. Even otherwise calm people sometimes find themselves turning into raving lunatics. When this happens, flames erupt.

A flame is a particularly nasty, personal attack on somebody for something he or she has written. Periodically, an exchange of flames erupts into a flame war that begins to take up all the space in a given newsgroup (and sometimes several; flamers like cross-posting to let the world know how they feel). These can go on for weeks (sometimes they go on for years, in which case they become "holy wars," usually on such topics as the relative merits of Macintoshes and IBM computers). Often, just when they're dying down, somebody new to the flame war reads all the messages, gets upset, and issues an urgent plea that the flame war be taken to e-mail so everybody else can get back to whatever the newsgroup's business is. All this usually does, though, is start a brand new flame war, in which this poor person comes under attack for daring to question the First Amendment, prompting others to jump on the attackers for impugning this poor soul. . . . You get the idea.

Every so often, a discussion gets so out of hand that somebody predicts that either the government will catch on and shut the whole thing down or somebody will sue to close down the network, or maybe even the wrath of God will smite everybody involved. This brings what has become an inevitable rejoinder from others who realize that the network is, in fact, a resilient creature that will not die easily: "Imminent death of Usenet predicted. Film at 11."

Flame wars can be tremendously fun to watch at first. They quickly grow boring, though. And wait until the first time you're attacked!

Flamers are not the only net.characters to watch out for.

Spewers assume that whatever they are particularly concerned about either really is of universal interest or should be rammed down the throats of people who don't seem to care—as frequently as possible. You can usually tell a spewer's work by the number of articles he posts in a day on the same subject and the number of newsgroups to which he then sends these articles—both can reach well into double digits. Often, these messages relate to various ethnic conflicts around the world. Frequently, there is no conceivable connection between the issue at hand and most of the newsgroups to which he posts. No matter. If you try to point this out in a response to one of these messages, you will be inundated with angry messages that either accuse you of being an insensitive racist/American/whatever or ignore your point entirely to bring up several hundred more lines of commentary on the perfidy of whoever it is the spewer thinks is out to destroy his people.

Closely related to these folks are the Holocaust revisionists, who periodically inundate certain groups (such as soc.history) with long rants about how the Holocaust never really happened. Some people attempt to refute these people with facts, but others realize this only encourages them.

Blatherers tend to be more benign. Their problem is that they just can't get to the point—they can wring three or four screenfuls out of a thought that others might sum up in a sentence or two. A related condition is excessive quoting. People afflicted with this will include an entire message in their reply rather than excising the portions not relevant to whatever point they're trying to make. The worst quote a long message and then add a single line:

```
"I agree!"
```

or some such, often followed by a monster .signature (see section 4.5).

There are a number of other Usenet denizens you'll soon come to recognize. Among them:

Net.weenies. These are the kind of people who enjoy insulting others, the kind of people who post nasty messages in a sewing newsgroup just for the hell of it.

Net.geeks. People to whom the Net is Life, who worry about what happens when they graduate and they lose their free, 24-hour access.

Net.gods. The old-timers; the true titans of the Net and the keepers of its collective history. They were around when the Net consisted of a couple of computers tied together with baling wire.

Lurkers. Actually, you can't tell these people are there, but they are. They're the folks who read a newsgroup but never post or respond.

Wizards. People who know a particular Net-related topic inside and out. Unix wizards can perform amazing tricks with that operating system, for example.

Net.saints. Always willing to help a newcomer, eager to share their knowledge with those not born with an innate ability to navigate the Net, they are not as rare as you might think. Post a question about something and you'll often be surprised how many responses you get.

The last group brings us back to the Net's oral tradition. With few written guides, people have traditionally learned their way around the Net by asking somebody, whether at the terminal next to them or on the Net itself. That tradition continues: if you have a question, ask.

Today, one of the places you can look for help is in the news.newusers.questions newsgroup, which, as its name suggests, is a place to learn more about Usenet. But be careful what you post. Some of the Usenet wizards there get cranky sometimes when they have to answer the same question over and over again. Oh, they'll eventually answer your question, but not before they tell you should have asked your host system administrator first or looked at the postings in news.announce.newusers.

4.2 Killfiles, the Cure for What Ails You

As you keep reading Usenet, you are going to run across things or people that really drive you nuts—or that you just get tired of seeing.

Killfiles are just the thing for you. When you start your newsreader, it checks to see if you have any lists of words, phrases, or names you don't want to see. If you do, then it blanks out any messages containing those words.

Such as cascades.

As you saw earlier, when you post a reply to a message and include parts of that message, the original lines show up with a > in front of them. Well, what if you reply to a reply? Then you get a >> in front of the line. And if you reply to that reply? You get >>>. Keep this up, and soon you get a triangle of >'s building up in your message.

There are people who like building up these triangles, or cascades. They'll "respond" to your message by deleting everything you've said, leaving only the "In message 123435, you said:" part and the last line of your message, to which they add a nonsensical retort. On and on they go until the triangle has reached the right end of the page. Then they try to expand the triangle by deleting one > with each new line. Whoever gets to finish this mega-triangle wins.

There is even a newsgroup just for such folks: alt.cascade. Unfortunately, cascaders would generally rather cascade in other newsgroups. Because it takes a lot of messages to build up a completed cascade, the targeted newsgroup soon fills up with these messages. Of course, if you complain, you'll be bombarded with messages about the First Amendment and artistic expression—or worse, with another cascade. The only thing you can do is ignore them, by setting up a killfile.

There are also certain newsgroups where killfiles will come in handy because of the way the newsgroups are organized. For example, readers of rec.arts.tv.soaps always use an acronym in their subject line for the show they're writing about (AMC, for example, for *All My Children*). This way, people who only want to read about *One Life to Live* can blank out all the messages about *The Young and the Restless* and all the others (to keep people from accidentally screening out messages that might contain the letters "gh" in them, *General Hospital* viewers always use "gh:" in their subject lines).

Both nn and rn let you create killfiles, but in different ways.

To create a killfile in nn, go into the newsgroup with the offending messages and type a capital K. You'll see this at the bottom of your screen:

```
AUTO (k)ill or (s)elect (CR => Kill subject 30 days)
```

If you hit return, nn will ask you which article's subject you're tired of. Chose one, and the article and any followups will disappear, and you won't see them again for 30 days.

If you type a lowercase k instead, you'll get this:

```
AUTO KILL on (s)ubject or (n)ame (s)
```

If you hit your S key or just enter, you'll see this:

```
KILL Subject: (=/)
```

Type in the name of the offending word or phrase and hit enter. You'll then be prompted

```
KILL in (g)roup 'eff.test' or in (a)ll groups (g)
```

except that the name of the group you see will be the one you're actually in at the moment. Because cascaders and other annoying people often cross-post their messages to a wide range of newsgroups, you might consider hitting a instead of g. Next comes this:

```
Lifetime of entry in days (p)ermanent (30)
```

The p key will screen out the offending articles forever, while hitting enter will do it for 30 days. You can also type in a number of days for the blocking.

Creating killfiles in rn works differently—its default killfile generator only works for messages in specific groups, rather than globally for your entire newsgroup list. To create a global killfile, you'll have to write one yourself.

To create a killfile in rn, go into the newsgroup where the offending messages are and type in its number so you get it on your screen. Type a capital K. From now on, any message with that subject line will disappear before you read the group. You should probably choose a reply, rather than the original message, so that you will get all of the followups (the original message won't have a "Re:" in its subject line). The next time you call up that newsgroup, rn will tell you it's killing messages. When it's done, hit the space bar to go back into reading mode.

To create a "global" killfile that will automatically wipe out articles in all groups you read, start rn and type control-K. This will start your whatever text editor you have as your default on your host system and create a file (called KILL, in your News subdirectory).

On the first line, you'll type in the word, phrase, or name you don't want to see, followed by commands that tell rn whether to search an entire message for the word or name and then what to do when it finds it.

Each line must be in this form:

```
/pattern/modifier:j
```

"Pattern" is the word or phrase you want rn to look for. It's case insensitive: both "test" and "Test" will be knocked out. The modifier tells rn whether to limit its search to message headers (which can be useful when the object is never to see messages from a particular person):

a   Looks through an entire message

h   Looks just at the header

You can leave out the modifier command, in which case rn will look only at the subject line of messages. The "j" at the end tells rn to screen out all articles with the offending word.

So if you never want to see the word "foo" in any header, ever again, type this:

```
/foo/h:j
```

This is particularly useful for getting rid of articles from people who post in more than one newsgroup, such as cascaders, since an article's newsgroup name is always in the header.

If you just want to block messages with a subject line about cascades, you could try:

```
/foo/:j
```

To kill anything that is a followup to any article, use this pattern:

```
/Subject: *Re:/:j
```

When done writing lines for each phrase to screen, exit the text editor as you normally would, and you'll be put back in rn.

One word of caution: go easy on the global killfile. An extensive global killfile, or one that makes frequent use of the a: modifier, can dramatically slow down rn, since the system will now have to look at every single word in every single message in all the newsgroups you want to read.

If there's a particular person whose posts you never want to see again, first find his or her address (which will be in the "from:" line of the postings) and then write a line in your killfile like this:

```
/From: *name@address\.all/h:j
```

4.3 Some Usenet Hints

Case counts in Unix—most of the time. Many Unix commands, including many of those used for reading Usenet articles, are case sensitive. Hit a d when you meant a D and either nothing will happen, or something completely different from what you expected will happen. So watch that case!

In nn, you can get help most of the time by typing a question mark (the exception is when you are writing your own message, because then you are inside the text-processing program). In rn, type a lower-case h at any prompt to get some online help.

When you're searching for a particular newsgroup, whether through the l command in rn or with nngrep for nn, you sometimes may have to try several keywords. For example, there is a newsgroup dedicated to the Grateful Dead, but you'd never find it if you tried, say, l grateful dead, because the name is rec.music.gdead. In general, try the smallest possible part of the word or discussion you're looking for, for example, use "trek" to find newsgroups about "Star Trek." If one word doesn't produce anything, try another.

4.4 The Brain Tumor Boy, the Modem Tax, and the Chain Letter

Like the rest of the world, Usenet has its share of urban legends and questionable activities. There are three in particular that plague the network. Spend more than, oh, 15 minutes within Usenet and you're sure to run into the Brain Tumor Boy, the plot by the evil FCC to tax your modem, and Dave Rhode's miracle cure for poverty. For the record, here's the story on all of them:

There once was a seven-year-old boy in England named Craig Shergold who was diagnosed with a seemingly incurable brain tumor. As he lay dying, he wished only to have friends send him postcards. The local newspapers got ahold of the tear-jerking story. Soon, the boy's wish had changed: he now wanted to get into the *Guinness Book of World Records* for the largest postcard collection. Word spread around the world. People by the millions sent him postcards.

Miraculously, the boy lived. An American billionaire even flew him to the United States for surgery to remove what remained of the tumor. And his wish succeeded beyond his wildest dreams—he made the *Guinness Book of World Records*.

But with Craig now well into his teens, his dream has turned into a nightmare for the post office in the small town outside London where he lives. Like Craig himself, his request for cards just refuses to die, inundating the post office with millions of cards every year. Just when it seems like the flow is slowing, along comes somebody else who starts up a whole new slew of requests for people to send Craig postcards (or greeting cards or business cards—Craig letters have truly taken on a life of their own and begun to mutate). Even Dear Abby has been powerless to make it stop!

What does any of this have to do with the Net? The Craig letter seems to pop up on Usenet as often as it does on cork boards at major corporations. No matter how many times somebody like Gene Spafford posts periodic messages to ignore them or spend your money on something more sensible (a donation to the local Red Cross, say), somebody manages to post a letter asking readers to send cards to poor little Craig.

Don't send any cards to the Federal Communications Commission, either.

In 1987, the FCC considered removing a tax break it had granted CompuServe and other large commercial computer networks for use of the national phone system. The FCC quickly reconsidered after alarmed users of bulletin board systems bombarded it with complaints about this "modem tax."

Now, every couple of months, somebody posts an "urgent" message warning Net users that the FCC is about to impose a modem tax. This is NOT true. The way you can tell if you're dealing with the hoax story is simple: it ALWAYS mentions an incident in which a talk-show host on KGO radio in San Francisco becomes outraged on the air while reading a story about the tax in the *New York Times*.

Another way to tell it's not true is that it never mentions a specific FCC docket number or closing date for comments.

Save that letter to your congressman for something else.

Sooner or later, you're going to run into a message titled "Make Money Fast." It's your basic chain letter. The Usenet version is always about some guy named Dave Rhodes who was on the verge of death, or something, when he discovered a perfectly legal way to make tons of money—by posting a chain letter on computer systems around the world. Yeah, right.

4.5 Big Sig

There are .sigs and there are .sigs. Many people put only bare-bones information in their .sig files—their names and e-mail addresses, perhaps their phone numbers. Others add a quotation they think is funny or profound and a disclaimer that their views are not those of their employer. Still others add some ASCII-art graphics. And then there are those who go totally berserk, posting huge creations with multiple quotes, hideous ASCII "barfics," and more e-mail addresses than anybody could humanly need. College freshmen unleashed on the Net seem to excel at these. You can see the best of the worst in the alt.fan.warlord newsgroup, which exists solely to critique .sigs that go too far, such as this one:

```
|###############################################################|
|#|                                                           |#|
|#|  *****   *     *  *****     *    *  *****  *****   *****    |#|
|#|    *     *     *  *        ** ** **  *      *         *   * |#|
|#|    *     ******  ***      *  *  *  ***    *  **  ***** **** |#|
|#|    *     *     *  *        *  *  *  *      *  *  *     *   * |#|
|#|    *     *     *  *****    *  *  *  ****  *****  *     *    |#|
|#|                                                           |#|
|#|  ****  *****  *****      *****  *****  *****     *****  *****|#|
|#|  *  **    *      *           *     *      *       *      *  *|#|
|#|  ***     *      *   **     *****    *     **      *      *  *|#|
|#|  * **    *      *    *      **      *     *       *      *  *|#|
|#|  ****  *****  *****   **  *****  *****  *****     *****  *****|#|
|#|                                                           |#|
|#|        T-H-E M-E-G-A B-I-G .S-I-G C-O-M-P-A-N-Y           |#|
|#|        ~--------------------------~                       |#|
|#|    "Annoying people with huge net.signatures for          |#|
|#|                over 20 years ..."                         |#|
|#|                                                           |#|
|#|-----------------------------------------------------------|#|
|#| "The difference between a net.idiot and a bucket of shit  |#|
|#| is that at least a bucket can be emptied. Let me further  |#|
|#| illustrate my point  by comparing these charts here.     |#|
|#| (pulls out charts) Here we have a user who not only       |#|
|#| flames people who don't agree with his narrow-minded      |#|
|#| drivel, but he has this huge signature that takes up many|#|
|#| pages with useless quotes. This also makes reading his    |#|
|#| frequented newsgroups a torture akin to having at 300     |#|
|#| baud modem on a VAX. I  might also add that his contri-   |#|
|#| bution to society rivals only toxic dump sites."          |#|
```

```
|#|                    —Robert A. Dumpstik, Jr                    |#|
|#|                  President of The Mega Big Sig Company         |#|
|#|                  September 13th, 1990 at 4:15pm                |#|
|#|                  During his speech at the "Net.abusers         |#|
|#|                  Society Luncheon" during the                  |#|
|#|                  "1990 Net.idiots Annual Convention"           |#|
|#|_____|#|
|#|                                                               |#|
|#| Thomas Babbit, III: 5th Assistant to the Vice                 |#|
|#| President of Sales                                            |#|
|#|     __                                                        |#|
|#| ==========    _____         Digital Widget Mfcturing Co.     |#|
|#|     \\      /                 1147 Complex Incorporated Dr.    |#|
|#|      )-=======                Suite 215                        |#|
|#|                               Nostromo, VA 22550-1147          |#|
|#| #NC-17 Enterpoop Ship :)      Phone # 804-844-2525             |#|
|#| -----------                   Fax # 804-411-1115              |#|
|#| "Shut up, Wesley!"            Online Service #804-411-1100    |#|
|#|               --Me            at 300-2400, and now            |#|
|#|                               9600 baud!                      |#|
|#|                               PUNet: tbabb!digwig!nostromo    |#|
|#| Home address:          InterNet: dvader@imperial.emp.com      |#|
|#| Thomas Babbit, III     Prodigy: Still awaiting author-        |#|
|#| 104 Luzyer Way                 ization                        |#|
|#| Sulaco, VA 22545       "Manufacturing educational widget      |#|
|#| Phone # 804-555-1524    design for over 3 years..."          |#|
|#|===============================================================|#|
|#|                                                               |#|
|#| Introducing:                                                  |#|
|#|                                                               |#|
|#|                              _____                           |#|
|#|The        |\ /|                  /                            |#|
|#|           | \/ |                /                             |#|
|#|           |    |               /                              |#|
|#|           |    |              /                               |#|
|#|           |    | ETELHED     /_____ ONE                      |#|
|#|'´`´`´`´`´`´`´`´`´`´`´`´`´`´`´`´`´`´`´`´`´`´`´`´`´`´`´`´`´`´`´`  |#|
|#| 50Megs Online! The k00l BBS for rad teens! Lots of games      |#|
|#| and many bases for kul topix! Call now and be validated       |#|
|#| to the Metelhed Zone|#|                                       |#|
|#|                  -804-555-8500-                               |#|
|#|\\\\\\\\\\\\\\\\\\\\\\\\\\\\\\\V//////////////////////////////  |#|
```

```
|#|  "This is the end, my friend . . ."  —The Doors              |#|
|###############################################################|
```

```
Hit "b" to continue
Hahahha . . . fooled u!
```

4.6 The First Amendment As Local Ordinance

Usenet's international reach raises interesting legal questions that have yet to be fully resolved. Can a discussion or posting that is legal in one country be transmitted to a country where it is against the law? Does the posting even become illegal when it reaches the border? And what if that country is the only path to a third country where the message is legal as well? Several foreign colleges and other institutions have cut off feeds of certain newsgroups where Americans post what are, in the United States, perfectly legal discussions of drugs or alternative sexual practices. Even in the United States, some universities have discontinued certain newsgroups their administrators find offensive, again, usually in the alt. hierarchy.

An interesting example of this sort of question happened in 1993, when a Canadian court issued a gag order on Canadian reporters covering a particularly controversial murder case. Americans, not bound by the gag order, began posting accounts of the trial—which any Canadian with a Net account could promptly read.

4.7 Usenet History

In the late 1970s, Unix developers came up with a new feature: a system to allow Unix computers to exchange data over phone lines.

In 1979, two graduate students at Duke University in North Carolina, Tom Truscott and Jim Ellis, came up with the idea of using this system, known as UUCP (for Unix-to-Unix CoPy), to distribute information of interest to people in the Unix community. Along with Steve Bellovin, a graduate student at the University of North Carolina, and Steve Daniel, another Duke graduate student, they wrote conferencing software and linked together computers at Duke and UNC.

Word quickly spread, and by 1981, a graduate student at Berkeley, Mark Horton, and a nearby high school student, Matt Glickman, had released a new version that added more features and was able to handle larger volumes of postings—the original North Carolina program was meant for only a few articles in a newsgroup each day.

Today, Usenet connects tens of thousands of sites around the world, from mainframes to Amigas. With more than 3,000 newsgroups and untold thousands of readers, it is perhaps the world's largest computer network.

4.8 When Things Go Wrong

• When you start up rn, you get a "warning" that "bogus newsgroups" are present. Within a couple of minutes, you'll be asked whether to keep these or delete them.

Delete them. Bogus newsgroups are newsgroups that your system administrator or somebody else has determined are no longer needed.

• While in a newsgroup in rn, you get a message: "skipping unavailable article."

This is usually an article that somebody posted and then decided to cancel.

• You upload a text file to your Unix host system for use in a Usenet message or e-mail, and when you or your recipient reads the file, every line ends with a ^M.

This happens because Unix handles line endings differently than MSDOS or Macintosh computers. Most Unix systems have programs to convert incoming files from other computers. To use it, upload your file and then, at your command line, type

```
dos2unix filename filename or

mac2unix filename filename
```

depending on which kind of computer you are using and where filename is the name of the file you've just uploaded. A similar program can prepare text files for downloading to your computer, for example

```
unix2dos filename filename or

unix2mac filename filename
```

will ensure that a text file you are about to get will not come out looking odd on your computer.

4.9 FYI

Leanne Phillips periodically posts a list of frequently asked questions (and answers) about use of the rn killfile function in the news.newusers.questions and news.answers newsgroups on Usenet. Bill Wohler posts a guide to using the nn newsreader in the news.answers and news.software newsgroups. Look in the news.announce.newusers and news.groups newsgroups on Usenet for "A Guide to Social Newsgroups and Mailing Lists," which gives brief summaries of the various soc. newsgroups.

Managing UUCP and Usenet, by Tim O'Reilly and Grace Todino (O'Reilly & Associates, 1992) is a good guide for setting up your own Usenet system.

5   Mailing Lists and Bitnet

5.1   Internet Mailing Lists

Usenet is not the only forum on the Net. Scores of "mailing lists" represent another way to interact with other Net users. Unlike Usenet messages, which are stored in one central location on your host system's computer, mailing-list messages are delivered right to your e-mail box.

You have to ask for permission to join a mailing list. Unlike Usenet, where your message is distributed to the world, on a mailing list you send your messages to a central moderator, who either remails it to the other people on the list or uses it to compile a periodic "digest" mailed to subscribers.

Given the number of newsgroups, why would anybody bother with a mailing list? Even on Usenet, there are some topics that just might not generate enough interest for a newsgroup; for example, the Queen list, which is all about the late Freddie Mercury's band.

And because a moderator decides who can participate, a mailing list can offer a degree of freedom to speak one's mind (or not worry about net.weenies) that is not necessarily possible on Usenet. Several groups offer anonymous postings—only the moderator knows the real names of people who contribute. Examples include 12Step, where people enrolled in such programs as Alcoholics Anonymous can discuss their experiences, and sappho, a list limited to gay and bisexual women.

You can find mailing addresses and descriptions of these lists in the news.announce.newusers newsgroup with the subject of "Publicly Accessible Mailing Lists." Mailing lists now number in the hundreds, so this posting is divided into three parts.

If you find a list to which you want to subscribe, send an e-mail message to

```
list-request@address
```

where "list" is the name of the mailing list and "address" is the moderator's e-mail address, asking to be added to the list. Include your full e-mail address just in case something happens to your message's header along the way, and ask, if you're accepted, for the address to mail messages to the list.

5.2 Bitnet

As if Usenet and mailing lists were not enough, there are Bitnet "discussion groups" or "lists."

Bitnet is an international network linking colleges and universities, but it uses a different set of technical protocols for distributing information from the Internet or Usenet. It offers hundreds of discussion groups, comparable in scope to Usenet newsgroups.

One of the major differences is the way messages are distributed. Bitnet messages are sent to your mailbox, just as with a mailing list. However, where mailing lists are often maintained by a person, all Bitnet discussion groups are automated—you subscribe to them through messages to a "listserver" computer. This is a kind of robot moderator that controls distribution of messages on the list. In many cases, it also maintains indexes and archives of past postings in a given discussion group, which can be handy if you want to get up to speed with a discussion or just search for some information related to it.

Many Bitnet discussion groups are now "translated" into Usenet form and carried through Usenet in the bit.listserv hierarchy. In general, it's probably better to read messages through Usenet if you can. It saves some storage space on your host system's hard drives.

If 50 people subscribe to the same Bitnet list, that means 50 copies of each message get stored on the system; whereas if 50 people read a Usenet message, that's still only one message that needs storage on the system. It can also save your sanity if the discussion group generates large numbers of messages. Think of opening your e-mailbox one day to find 200 messages in it—199 of them from a discussion group and one of them a "real" e-mail message that's important to you.

Subscribing and canceling subscriptions is done through an e-mail message to the listserver computer. For addressing, all listservers are known as "listserv" (yep) at some Bitnet address. This means you will have to add ".bitnet" to the end of the address, if it's in a form like this: listserv@miamiu. For example, if you have an interest in environmental issues, you might want to subscribe to the Econet discussion group. To subscribe, send an e-mail message to the following address:

```
listserv@miamiu.bitnet
```

Some Bitnet listservers are also connected to the Internet, so if you see a listserver address ending in ".edu," you can e-mail the listserver without adding ".bitnet" to the end.

Always leave the "subject:" line blank in a message to a listserver. Inside the message, you tell the listserver what you want, with a series of simple commands:

subscribe group Your Name	To subscribe to a list, where "group" is the list name and "Your Name" is your full name, for example:
	```subscribe econet Henry Fielding```
unsubscribe group Your Name	To discontinue a group
	```unsubscribe econet Henry Fielding```
list global	This sends you a list of all available Bitnet discussion groups. But be careful—the list is VERY long!
get refcard	Sends you a list of other commands you can use with a listserver

Each of these commands goes on a separate line in your message (and you can use one or all of them). If you want to get a list of all Bitnet discussion groups, send e-mail to

```
listserv@bitnic.educom.edu
```

Leave the "subject:" line blank and use the list global command.

When you subscribe to a Bitnet group, you need to know two important differences from Usenet.

First, when you want to post a message for others to read in the discussion group, you send a message to the group name at its Bitnet

address. Using Econet as an example, you would mail the message to
this address:

```
econet@miamiu.bitnet
```

Note that this is different from the listserv address you used to
subscribe to the group to begin with. Use the listserv address ONLY
to subscribe to or unsubscribe from a discussion group. If you use the
discussion-group address to try to subscribe or unsubscribe, your
message will go out to every other subscriber, many of whom will
think unkind thoughts, which they may share with you in an e-mail
message.

The second difference relates to sending an e-mail message to the
author of a particular posting. Usenet newsreaders such as rn and nn
let you do this with one key. But if you hit your R key to respond to
a discussion-group message, your message will go to the listserver,
and from there to everybody else on the list! This can prove embar-
rassing to you and annoying to others. To make sure your message
goes just to the person who wrote the posting, take down the author's
e-mail address from the posting and then compose a brand-new message. Remember, also, that if you see an e-mail address like IZZY@
INDYVMS, it's a Bitnet address.

Two Bitnet lists will prove helpful for delving further into the network. NEW-LIST tells you the names of new discussion groups. To
subscribe, send a message to listserv@ndsuvm1.bitnet:

```
sub NEW-LIST Your Name
```

INFONETS is the place to go when you have questions about Bitnet.
It is also first rate for help on questions about all major computer
networks and how to reach them. To subscribe, send e-mail to info-
nets-request@think.com:

```
sub INFONETS Your Name
```

Both of these lists are also available on Usenet, the former as bit.list-
serv.new-list; the latter as bit.listserv.infonets (sometimes bit.list-
serv.info-nets).

6 Telnet

6.1 Mining the Net

Like any large community, cyberspace has its libraries, places you can go to look up information or take out a good book. Telnet is one of your keys to these libraries.

Telnet is a program that lets you use the power of the Internet to connect to databases, library catalogs, and other information resources around the world. Want to see what the weather's like in Vermont? Check on crop conditions in Azerbaijan? Get more information about somebody whose name you've seen online? Telnet lets you do this, and more.

Alas, there's a big "but"! Unlike the phone system, Internet is not yet universal; not everybody can use all of its services. Almost all colleges and universities on the Internet provide telnet access. So do all of the for-fee public-access systems listed in chapter 1. But the Free-Net systems do not give you access to every telnet system. And if you are using a public-access UUCP or Usenet site, you will not have access to telnet. The main reason for this is cost. Connecting to the Internet can easily cost $1,000 or more for a leased, high-speed phone line. Some databases and file libraries can be queried by e-mail, however; we'll show you how to do that later on. In the meantime, the rest of this chapter assumes you are connected to a site with at least partial Internet access.

Most telnet sites are fairly easy to use and have online help systems. Most also work best (and in some cases, only) with VT100 emulation. Let's dive right in and try one.

At your host system's command line, type

```
telnet access.usask.ca
```

and hit enter. That's all you have to do to connect to a telnet site! In this case, you'll be connecting to a service known as Hytelnet, which is a database of computerized library catalogs and other databases available through telnet. You should see something like this:

```
Trying 128.233.3.1 . . .
Connected to access.usask.ca.
Escape character is '^]'.

Ultrix UNIX (access.usask.ca)

login:
```

Every telnet site has two addresses—one is composed of words that are easier for people to remember; the other is a numerical address better suited for computers. The "escape character" is good to remember. When all else fails, hitting your control key and the] key at the same time will disconnect you and return you to your host system. At the login prompt, type

```
hytelnet
```

and hit enter. You'll see something like this:

```
                    Welcome to HYTELNET
                       version 6.2

                  . . . . . . . . . . . . . . . . . .

What is HYTELNET?        <WHATIS>      Up/Down arrows MOVE
Library catalogs        <SITES1>    . Left/Right arrows SELECT
Other resources         <SITES2>    . ? for HELP anytime
Help files for catalogs <OP000>
Catalog interfaces      <SYS000>    . m returns here
Internet Glossary       <GLOSSARY>  . q quits
Telnet tips             <TELNET>
Telnet/TN3270 escape    <ESCAPE.KEY> .
   keys
Key-stroke commands     <HELP.TXT>      .

                  . . . . . . . . . . . . . . . . . . . . . . . . .
                    HYTELNET 6.2 was written by Peter Scott,
        U of Saskatchewan Libraries, Saskatoon, Sask, Canada. 1992
Unix and VMS software by Earl Fogel, Computing Services, U of S
1992
```

The first choice, "<WHATIS>," will be highlighted. Use your down and up arrows to move the cursor among the choices. Hit enter when you decide on one. You'll get another menu, which in turn will bring up text files telling you how to connect to sites and giving any special commands or instructions you might need. Hytelnet does have one quirk. To move back to where you started (for example, from a sub-menu to a main menu), hit the left-arrow key on your computer.

Play with the system. You might want to turn on your computer's screen capture, or at the very least, get out a pen and paper. You're bound to run across some interesting telnet services that you'll want to try—and you'll need their telnet "addresses."

As you move around Hytelnet, it may seem as if you haven't left your host system—telnet can work that quickly. Occasionally, when network loads are heavy, however, you will notice a delay between the time you type a command or enter a request and the time the remote service responds.

To disconnect from Hytelnet and return to your system, hit your q key and enter.

Some telnet computers are set up so that you can only access them through a specific "port." In those cases, you'll always see a number after their name, for example: india.colorado.edu 13. It's important to include that number, because otherwise, you may not get in.

In fact, try the previous address. Type

```
telnet india.colorado.edu 13
```

and hit enter. You should see something like this:

```
Trying 128.138.140.44 . . .
```

Followed very quickly by this:

```
telnet india.colorado.edu 13

Escape character is '^]'.
Sun Jan 17 14:11:41 1994
Connection closed by foreign host.
```

What we want is the middle line, which tells you the exact mountain standard time, as determined by a government-run atomic clock in Boulder, Colorado.

6.2 Library Catalogs

Several hundred libraries around the world, from the Snohomish Public Library in Washington State to the Library of Congress, are now available to you through telnet. You can use Hytelnet to find their names, telnet addresses, and use instructions.

Why would you want to browse a library you can't physically get to? Many libraries share books, so if yours doesn't have what you're looking for, you can tell the librarian where he or she can get it. Or if you live in an area where the libraries are not yet online, you can use telnet to do some basic bibliographic research before you head down to the local branch.

There are several different database programs in use by online libraries. Harvard's is one of the easier ones to use, so let's try it.

Telnet to hollis.harvard.edu. When you connect, you'll see this:

```
****************  H A R V A R D   U N I V E R S I T Y
***************   OFFICE FOR INFORMATION TECHNOLOGY
***      ***     ***
*** VE *** RI ***
***      ***     ***  HOLLIS (Harvard OnLine LIbrary System)
  *****       *****
   **** TAS ****      HUBS (Harvard University Basic Services)
    ***     ***
       *****          IU (Information Utility)
        ***

                     CMS (VM/CMS Timesharing Service)


   ** HOLLIS IS AVAILABLE WITHOUT ACCESS RESTRICTIONS **
Access to other applications is limited to individuals
who have been granted specific permission by an author-
ized person.

To select one of the applications above, type its name
on the command line followed by your user ID, and press
RETURN.

           ** HOLLIS DOES NOT REQUIRE A USERID **
EXAMPLES: HOLLIS (press RETURN) or HUBS userid
(press RETURN)
===>
```

Type

```
hollis
```

and hit enter. You'll see several screens flash by quickly until finally
the system stops and you'll get this:

```
              WELCOME TO HOLLIS
      (Harvard OnLine Library Information System)
To begin, type one of the 2-character database codes
listed below:
   HU   Union Catalog of the Harvard libraries
   OW   Catalog of Older Widener materials
   LG   Guide to Harvard Libraries and Computing Resources

   AI   Expanded Academic Index (selective 1987-1988,
        full 1989- )
   LR   Legal Resource Index (1980- )
   PA   PAIS International (1985- )

To change databases from any place in HOLLIS, type
CHOOSE followed by a 2-character database code, as in:
CHOOSE HU

For general help in using HOLLIS, type HELP. For HOLLIS
news, type HELP NEWS. For HOLLIS hours of operation,
type HELP HOURS.

       ALWAYS PRESS THE ENTER OR RETURN KEY AFTER
                TYPING YOUR COMMAND
```

   The first thing to notice is the name of the system: Hollis. Librarians
around the world seem to be inordinately found of cutesy, anthropo-
morphized acronyms for their machines (not far from Harvard, the
librarians at Brandeis University came up with Library On-Line User
Information Service, or Louis; MIT has Barton).
   If you want to do some general browsing, probably the best bet on
the Harvard system is to chose HU, which gets you access to their
main holdings, including those of the medical libraries. Chose that,
and you'll see this:

```
    THE HARVARD UNIVERSITY LIBRARY UNION CATALOG
To begin a search, select a search option from the list
below and type its code on the command line. Use either
upper or lower case.
```

```
AU        Author search
TI        Title search
SU        Subject search
ME        Medical subject search
KEYWORD   Keyword search options
CALL      Call number search options
OTHER     Other search options
```

For information on the contents of the Union Catalog,
type HELP. To exit the Union Catalog, type QUIT.

A search can be entered on the COMMAND line of any
screen.

        ALWAYS PRESS THE ENTER OR RETURN KEY AFTER TYPING
YOUR COMMAND.

Say you want to see if Harvard has shed the starchy legacy of the
Puritans, who founded the school. Why not see if they have *The Joy of
Sex* somewhere in their stacks? Type

```
TI Joy of Sex
```

and hit enter. This comes up:

```
HU: YOUR SEARCH RETRIEVED NO ITEMS. Enter new command or
HELP.You typed:
 TI JOY OF SEX


*************************************************************



*ALWAYS PRESS THE ENTER OR RETURN KEY AFTER TYPING YOUR
COMMAND.
------------------------------------------------------------
OPTIONS: FIND     START - search options        HELP
                  QUIT  - exit database
COMMAND?
```

Oh, well! Do they have anything that mentions "sex" in the title? Try
another TI search, but this time just type "TI sex." You get:

```
HU GUIDE: SUMMARY OF SEARCH RESULTS 2086 items retrieved
by your search:
```

```
FIND TI SEX
------------------------------------------------------------
   1 SEX
   2 SEX A
 823 SEXA
 827 SEXBO
 831 SEXCE
 833 SEXDR
 834 SEXE
 879 SEXIE
 928 SEXJA
 929 SEXLE
 930 SEXO
 965 SEXPI
 968 SEXT
1280 SEXUA
2084 SEXWA
2085 SEXY
------------------------------------------------------------
OPTIONS: INDEX (or I 5 etc) to see list of items  HELP
                                        START - search options
     REDO - edit search          QUIT  - exit database
COMMAND?
```

If you want to get more information on the first line, type 1 and hit enter:

```
HU INDEX: LIST OF ITEMS RETRIEVED 2086 items retrieved
by your search:
FIND TI SEX
-------------------------------------------------
SEX
     1 geddes patrick sir 1854 1932/ 1914 bks

SEX A Z
     2 goldenson robert m/ 1987 bks

SEX ABUSE HYSTERIA SALEM WITCH TRIALS REVISITED
     3 gardner richard a/ 1991 bks

SEX AETATES MUNDI ENGLISH AND IRISH
     4 irish sex aetates mundi/ 1983 bks
```

```
SEX AFTER SIXTY A GUIDE FOR MEN AND WOMEN FOR THEIR
LATER YEARS
     5 butler robert n 1927/ 1976 bks


----------------------------------------(CONTINUES)--
OPTIONS: DISPLAY 1 (or D 5 etc) to see a record HELP
     GUIDE       MORE - next page    START - search options
     REDO - edit search              QUIT - exit database
COMMAND?
```

Most library systems give you a way to log off and return to your host system. On Hollis, hit escape followed by this command:

```
xx
```

One particularly interesting system is the one run by the Colorado Alliance of Research Libraries, which maintains databases for libraries throughout Colorado, the west, and even in Boston.

```
Telnet pac.carl.org.
```

Follow the simple log-in instructions. When you get a menu, type 124 (even though that is not listed), which takes you to the Pikes Peak Library District, which serves the city of Colorado Springs.

Several years ago, its librarians realized they could use their database program not just for books but for cataloging city records and community information, as well. Today, if you want to look up municipal ordinances or city records, you only have to type in the word you're looking for and you'll get back cites of the relevant laws or decisions.

Carl will also connect you to the University of Hawaii library, which, like the one in Colorado Springs, has more than just bibliographic material online. One of its features is an online Hawaiian almanac that can tell you everything you ever wanted to know about Hawaiians, including the number injured in boogie-board accidents each year (seven).

6.3 Some Interesting Telnet Sites

Agriculture

PENPages, run by Pennsylvania State University's College of Agricultural Sciences, provides weekly world weather and crop reports from the U.S. Department of Agriculture. These reports detail everything from the effect of the weather on palm trees in Malaysia to the state of the Ukrainian wheat crop. Reports from Pennsylvania country extension officers offer tips for improving farm life. One database lists Pennsylvania hay distributors by county—and rates the quality of their hay!

The service lets you search for information two different ways. A menu system gives you quick access to reports that change frequently, such as the weekly crop/weather reports. An index system lets you search through several thousand online documents by keyword. At the main menu, you can either browse through an online manual or chose "PENPages," which puts you into the agriculture system.

Telnet: psupen.psu.edu

User name: Your two-letter state code or WORLD

California State University's **Advanced Technology Information Network** provides similar information as PENPages, only focusing on California crops. It also maintains lists of upcoming California trade shows and carries updates on biotechnology.

Telnet: caticsuf.cati.csufresno.edu

Log in: public

You will then be asked to register and will be given a user name and password. Hit "a" at the main menu for agricultural information. Hit "d" to call up a menu that includes a biweekly biotechnology report.

AIDS

The **University of Miami** maintains a database of AIDS health providers in southern Florida.

Telnet: callcat.med.miami.edu

Log in: library

At the main menu, select P (for "AIDS providers"), and you'll be able to search for doctors, hospitals, and other providers that care for patients with AIDS. You can also search by speciality.

See also Conversation and Health.

Amateur Radio

The **National Ham Radio Call-Sign Callbook** lets you search for American amateur operators by callsign, city, last name, or zip code. A successful search will give you the ham's name, address, callsign, age, type of license, and when he or she got it.
Telnet: callsign.cs.buffalo.edu 2000 or ham.njit.edu 2000.
When you connect, you tell the system how you want to search and what you're looking for. For example, if you want to search for hams by city, you would type

```
city city name
```

and hit enter (for example: city Kankakee).
Other search choices are "call" (after which you would type a ham's name), "name," and "zip" (which you would follow with a zip code). Be careful when searching for hams in a large city; there doesn't seem to be any way to shut off the list once it starts except by using control-]. Otherwise, when done, type

```
quit
```

and hit enter to disconnect.

Animals

See Health.

Calculators

Hewlett-Packard maintains a free service on which you can seek advice about their line of calculators.
Telnet: hpcvbbs.cv.hp.com
No log-in is needed.

Chemistry

The **Electronic Periodic Table of the Elements** draws the table on your screen and then lets you look up various properties of individual elements.
Telnet: camms2.caos.kun.nl
No password needed.

Congress

The **Library of Congress Information Service** lets you search current and past legislation (dating to 1982).

Telnet: locis.loc.gov

Password: none needed.

When you connect, you'll get a main menu that lets you select from several databases, including the Library of Congress card catalog (with book entries dating to 1978) and a database of information on copyright laws.

For the congressional database, select the number next to its entry and hit enter. You'll then be asked to choose which legislative year to search. After that, a menu similar to this will come up:

```
***C103- THE LEGISLATIVE INFORMATION FILE FOR THE 103RD
   CONGRESS, which was updated on 05/10/93 and contains
   4,044 records, is now available for your search.

   CURRENCY:All information is NOT current through the
      above date, which is machine generated when ANY in-
      formation is added to the file.Bill numbers, offi-
      cial titles, sponsors, and status (STEP) added
      within 48 hours. Indexing terms and digests added
      later, in some cases several weeks after the bill
      is added to the file.

   TO START  RETRIEVE to find:   EXAMPLES:
   SEARCH: member name -------->  retrieve rep gingrich
                                  retrieve sen kennedy
   bill number  --------------->  retrieve h.r. 1
   subject keywords ---------->   retrieve day care

FOR HELP: Type the word HELP and press the ENTER key.

READY FOR NEW COMMAND:
```

Conversation

Communications Canada, a Canadian government agency, is developing **Conversational Hypertext Access Technology (CHAT)** to provide easy database access to people with little or no computer experience, using what are known as hypertext links. Instead of cryptic computer commands, users type questions in English.

Telnet: debra.doc.ca

Log in: chat

You chose one of the three databases now online, one on AIDS, and then ask questions in English.

Ask the AIDS database, "When was AIDS first discovered?" and it answers, "The first case of AIDS in North America was diagnosed in 1979. Before that, it existed in Africa, probably beginning in the 1950's. AIDS was discovered in North America when a number of young men with a history of homosexuality developed a rare type of cancer called Kaposi's sarcoma."

Sometimes, you do have to rephrase your question. For example, when asked "What is the link between AIDS and drug use?" the computer responds, "I know two things about drugs: the drugs that are used to treat people with AIDS, and the risks that drug users have in getting AIDS. Please ask about treatments or drug users."

Copyright Law

See Congress.

Current Events

Every year, the **CIA publishes a Fact Book** that is essentially an almanac of all the world's countries and international organizations, including such information as major products, type of government, and names of its leaders. It's available for searching through the University of Maryland Info Database.

Telnet: info.umd.edu

Choose a terminal type and hit enter (or just hit enter if you are using VT100). At the main menu, choose the number next to "Educational Resources." Then select the number next to "International," followed by "Factbook." You can then search by country or agency.

This site also maintains copies of the U.S. budget, documents related to the North American Free Trade Agreement, and other government initiatives. At the "Educational Resources" menu, select the number next to "United States" and then the one next to "Government."

The **Access Legislative Information Service** lets you browse through and look up bills before the Hawaiian legislature.

Telnet: access.uhcc.hawaii.edu

Environment

Envirolink is a large database and conference system about the environment, based in Pittsburgh.
    Telnet: envirolink.org
    Log on: gopher

The **U.S. Environmental Protection Agency** maintains online databases of materials related to hazardous waste, the Clean Lakes program, and cleanup efforts in New England. The agency plans eventually to include cleanup work in other regions, as well. The database is actually a computerized card catalog of EPA documents—you can look the documents up, but you'll still have to visit your regional EPA office to see them.
    Telnet: epaibm.rtpnc.epa.gov
    No password or user name is needed. At the main menu, type

```
public
```

and hit enter (there are other listed choices, but they are only for use by EPA employees). You'll then see a one-line menu. Type

```
ols
```

and hit enter, and you'll see something like this:

```
NET-106 Logon to TSO04      in progress.

    DATABASES:
        N   NATIONAL CATALOG    CH   CHEMICAL COLL. SYSTEM
        H   HAZARDOUS WASTE      1   REGION I
        L   CLEAN LAKES

    OTHER OPTIONS:
        ?   HELP
        Q   QUIT

ENTER SELECTION->
```

    Choose one and you'll get a menu that lets you search by document title, keyword, year of publication, or corporation. After you enter the search word and hit enter, you'll be told how many matches were found. Hit 1 and then enter to see a list of the entries. To view the bibliographic record for a specific entry, hit V and enter and then type the number of the record.

The **University of Michigan** maintains a database of newspaper and magazine articles related to the environment, with the emphasis on Michigan, dating back to 1980.
Telnet: hermes.merit.edu
Host: mirlyn
Log in: meem

Geography

The **University of Michigan Geographic Name Server** can provide basic information, such as population, latitude, and longitude of U.S. cities and many mountains, rivers, and other geographic features.
Telnet: martini.eecs.umich.edu 3000

No password or user name is needed. Type in the name of a city, a zip code, or a geographic feature and hit enter. The system doesn't like names with abbreviations in them (for example, Mt. McKinley), so spell them out (for example, Mount McKinley).

By typing in a town's name or zip code, you can find out a community's county, zip code, and longitude and latitude. Not all geographic features are yet included in the database.

Government

The **National Technical Information Service** runs a system that not only provides huge numbers of federal documents of all sorts—from environmental factsheets to patent abstracts—but serves as a gateway to dozens of other federal information systems.
Telnet: fedworld.gov
Log on as: new

See also Congress and Current Events.

Health

The **U.S. Food and Drug Administration** runs a database of health-related information.

Telnet: fdabbs.fda.gov

Log in: bbs

You'll then be asked for your name and a password you want to use in the future. After that, type

```
topics
```

and hit enter. You'll see this:

```
TOPICS DESCRIPTION
* NEWS        News releases
* ENFORCE     Enforcement Report
* APPROVALS   Drug and Device Product Approvals list
* CDRH        Centers for Devices and Radiological Health
              Bulletins
* BULLETIN    Text from Drug Bulletin
* AIDS        Current Information on AIDS
* CONSUMER    FDA Consumer magazine index and selected
              articles
* SUBJ-REG    FDA Federal Register Summaries by Subject
* ANSWERS     Summaries of FDA information
* INDEX       Index of News Releases and Answers
* DATE-REG    FDA Federal Register Summaries by
              Publication Date
* CONGRESS    Text of Testimony at FDA Congressional
              Hearings
* SPEECH      Speeches Given by FDA Commissioner and
              Deputy
* VETNEWS     Veterinary Medicine News
* MEETINGS    Upcoming FDA Meetings
* IMPORT      Import Alerts
* MANUAL      On-Line User's Manual
```

You'll be able to search these topics by key word or chronologically. It's probably a good idea, however, to capture a copy of the manual first, because the way searching works on the system is a little odd. To capture a copy, type

```
manual
```

and hit enter. Then type

```
scan
```

and hit enter. You'll see this:

```
FOR LIST OF AVAILABLE TOPICS TYPE TOPICS
OR ENTER THE TOPIC YOU DESIRE ==>

MANUAL
BBSUSER
08-OCT-91
1 BBS User Manual
```

At this point, turn on your own computer's screen capture or logging function and hit your 1 key and then enter. The manual will begin to scroll on your screen, pausing every 24 lines.

Hiring and College Program Information

The **Federal Information Exchange** in Gaithersburg, Maryland, runs two systems at the same address: FEDIX and MOLIS. FEDIX offers research, scholarship, and service information for several federal agencies, including NASA, the Department of Energy, and the Federal Aviation Administration. Several more federal agencies provide minority hiring and scholarship information. MOLIS provides information about minority colleges, their programs, and professors.

Telnet: fedix.fie.com

User name: fedix (for the federal hiring database) or molis (for the minority-college system)

Both use easy menus to get you to information.

History

Stanford University maintains a database of documents related to Martin Luther King.

Telnet: forsythetn.stanford.edu

Account: socrates

At the main menu, type

```
select mlk
```

and hit enter.

Ski Reports

See Weather.

Space

NASA Spacelink in Huntsville, Alabama, provides all sorts of reports and data about NASA, its history, and its various missions, past and present. You'll find detailed reports on every single probe, satellite, and mission NASA has ever launched along with daily updates and lesson plans for teachers.

The system maintains a large file library of GIF-format space graphics, but you can't download these through telnet. If you want them, you have to dial the system directly, at (205) 895-0028.

Telnet: spacelink.msfc.nasa.gov

When you connect, you'll be given an overview of the system and asked to register and chose a password.

The **NED-NASA/IPAC Extragalactic Database** lists data on more than 100,000 galaxies, quasars, and other objects outside the Milky Way.

Telnet: ipac.caltech.edu

Log in: ned

You can learn more than you ever wanted to about quasars, novae, and related objects on a system run by the **Smithsonian Astrophysical Observatory** in Cambridge, Massachusetts.

Telnet: cfa204.harvard.edu

Log in: einline

The **physics department at the University of Massachusetts at Amherst** runs a bulletin board system that provides extensive conferences and document libraries related to space.

Telnet: spacemet.phast.umass.edu

Log on with your name and a password.

Supreme Court Decisions

The **University of Maryland Info Database** maintains U.S. Supreme Court decisions from 1991 on.

Telnet: info.umd.edu

Chose a terminal type and hit enter (or just hit enter if you are using VT100). At the main menu, choose the number next to "Educational Resources" and hit enter. One of your options will then be for "United States." Select that number and then, at the next menu, choose the one next to "Supreme Court."

Telnet

Hytelnet, at the University of Saskatchewan, is an online guide to hundreds of telnet sites around the world.
Telnet: access.usask.ca
Log in: hytelnet

Time

To find out the exact time:
Telnet: india.colorado.edu 13
You'll see something like this:

```
Escape character is '^]'.
Sun Apr 5 14:11:41 1992
Connection closed by foreign host.
```

The middle line tells you the date and exact mountain standard time, as determined by a federal atomic clock.

Transportation

The **Subway Navigator** in Paris can help you learn how long it will take to get from point A to point B on subway systems around the world.
Telnet: metro.jussieu.fr 10000
No log-in is needed.
When you connect, you'll be asked to choose a language in which to search (you can choose English or French) and then a city to search. You'll be asked for the station you plan to leave from and the station you want to get to.

Weather

The **University of Michigan's Department of Atmospheric, Oceano-graphic, and Space Sciences** supplies weather forecasts for U.S. and foreign cities, along with skiing and hurricane reports.
Telnet: madlab.sprl.umich.edu 3000 (note the 3000).
No log-in name is needed.
Also see Weather in the ftp list for information on downloading satellite and radar weather images.

6.4 Telnet Bulletin Board Systems

You might think that Usenet, with its hundreds of newsgroups, would be enough to satisfy the most dedicated of online communicators.

But there are a number of "bulletin board" and other systems that provide even more conferences or other services, many not found directly on the Net. Some are free; others charge for access. They include the following:

Bookstacks Unlimited is a Cleveland bookstore that uses the Internet to advertise its services. Its online system features not only a catalog, however, but conferences on books and literature.

Telnet: books.com

Log in with your own name and select a password for future connections.

Cimarron. Run by the Instituto Technical in Monterey, Mexico, this system has Spanish conferences, but English commands, as you can see from this menu of available conferences:

```
List of Boards
    Name              Title
    General           Board general
    Dudas             Dudas de Cimarron
    Comentarios       Comentarios al SYSOP
    Musica            Para los afinados. . . . . . . .
    Libros            El sano arte de leer. . . . .
    Sistemas          Sistemas Operativos en General.
    Virus             Su peor enemigo. . . . . .
    Cultural          Espacio Cultural de Cimarron
    NeXT              El Mundo de NeXT
    Ciencias          Solo apto para Nerds.
    Inspiracion       Para los Romanticos e Inspirados.
    Deportes          Discusiones Deportivas
```

To be able to write messages and gain access to files, you have to leave a note to SYSOP with your name, address, occupation, and phone number. To do this, at any prompt, hit your M key and then enter, which will bring up the mail system. Hitting H brings up a list of commands and how to use them.

Telnet: bugs.mty.itesm.mx (8 P.M. to 10 A.M., eastern time, only).

At the "login:" prompt, type

```
bbs
```

and hit enter.

Cleveland Free-Net. The first of a series of Free-Nets, this represents an ambitious attempt to bring the Net to the public. Originally an in-hospital help network, it is now sponsored by Case Western Reserve University, the city of Cleveland, the state of Ohio, and IBM. It uses simple menus, similar to those found on CompuServe, but organized like a city:

```
<<< CLEVELAND FREE-NET DIRECTORY >>>

 1 The Administration Building
 2 The Post Office
 3 Public Square
 4 The Courthouse & Government Center
 5 The Arts Building
 6 Science and Technology Center
 7 The Medical Arts Building
 8 The Schoolhouse (Academy One)
 9 The Community Center & Recreation Area
10 The Business and Industrial Park
11 The Library
12 University Circle
13 The Teleport
14 The Communications Center
15 NPTN/USA TODAY HEADLINE NEWS
----------------------------------------
h=Help, x=Exit Free-Net, "go help"=extended help

Your Choice ==>
```

The system has a vast and growing collection of public documents, from copies of U.S. and Ohio Supreme Court decisions to the Magna Carta and the U.S. Constitution. It links residents to various government agencies and has daily stories from *USA Today*. Beyond Usenet (found in the Teleport area), it has a large collection of local conferences on everything from pets to politics. And yes, it's free!

Telnet: freenet-in-a.cwru.edu or freenet-in-b.cwru.edu or freenet-in-c.cwru.edu

When you connect to Free-Net, you can look around the system. However, if you want to be able to post messages in its conferences or use e-mail, you will have to apply in writing for an account. Information on this is available when you connect.

DUBBS. This is a bulletin board system in Delft in the Netherlands. The conferences and files are mostly in Dutch, but the help files and the system commands themselves are in English.

Telnet: tudrwa.tudelft.nl

ISCA BBS. Run by the Iowa Student Computer Association, it has more than a hundred conferences, including several in foreign languages. After you register, hit K for a list of available conferences and then J to join a particular conference (you have to type in the name of the conference, not the number next to it). Hitting H brings up information about commands.

Telnet bbs.isca.uiowa.edu

At the "login:" prompt, type

```
bbs
```

and hit enter.

Youngstown Free-Net. The people who created Cleveland Free-Net sell their software for $1 to anybody willing to set up a similar system. A number of cities now have their own Free-Nets, including Youngstown, Ohio.

Telnet: yfn.ysu.edu At the "login:" prompt, type

```
visitor
```

and hit enter.

6.5 Putting the Finger on Someone

Finger is a handy little program that lets you find out more about people on the Net—and lets you tell others on the Net more about yourself.

Finger uses the same concept as telnet or ftp. But it works with only one file, called .plan (yes, with a period in front). This is a text file Internet users create with a text editor in their home directory. You can put your phone number in there, tell a little bit about yourself, or write almost anything at all.

To finger somebody else's .plan file, type this at the command line:

```
finger email-address
```

where email-address is the person's e-mail address. You'll get back a display that shows the last time the person was online, whether they've gotten any new mail since that time, and what, if anything, is in their .plan file.

Some people and institutions have come up with creative uses for these .plan files, letting you do everything from checking the weather in Massachusetts to getting the latest baseball standings. Try fingering these e-mail addresses:

weather@cirrus.mit.edu	Latest National Weather Service weather forecasts for regions in Massachusetts.
quake@geophys.washington.edu	Locations and magnitudes of recent earthquakes around the world.
jtchern@ocf.berkeley.edu	Current major-league baseball standings and results of the previous day's games.
nasanews@space.mit.edu	The day's events at NASA.
coke@cs.cmu.edu	See how many cans of each type of soda are left in a particular soda machine in the computer science department of Carnegie-Mellon University.

6.6 Finding Someone on the Net

So you have a friend and you want to find out if he has an Internet account to which you can write? The quickest way may be to just pick up the phone, call him, and ask him. Although there are a variety of "white pages" services available on the Internet, they are far from complete—college students, users of commercial services such as CompuServe and many Internet public-access sites, and many others simply won't be listed. Major e-mail providers are working on a universal directory system, but that could be some time away.

In the meantime, a couple of "white pages" services might give you some leads, or even just entertain you as you look up famous people or long-lost acquaintances.

The whois directory provides names, e-mail and postal mail addresses, and often phone numbers for people listed in it. To use it, telnet to this address:

```
internic.net
```

No log-on is needed. The quickest way to use it is to type

```
whois name
```

at the prompt, where "name" is the last name or organization name you're looking for.

Another service worth trying, especially since it seems to give beginners fewer problems, is the Knowbot Information Service reachable by telnet at

```
info.cnri.reston.va.us 185
```

Again, no log-on is needed. This service actually searches through a variety of other "white pages" systems, including the user directory for MCIMail. To look for somebody, type

```
query name
```

where "name" is the last name of the person you're looking for. You can get details of other commands by hitting a question mark at the prompt. You can also use the knowbot system by e-mail. Start a message to

```
netaddress@info.cnri.reston.va.us
```

You can leave the "subject:" line blank. As your message, type

```
query name
```

for the simplest type of search. If you want details on more complex searches, add another line:

```
man
```

Another way to search is via the Usenet name server. This is a system at MIT that keeps track of the e-mail addresses of everybody who posts a Usenet message that appears at MIT. It works by e-mail. Send a message to this address:

```
mail-server@rtfm.mit.edu
```

Leave the "subject:" line blank. As your message, write

```
send usenet-addresses/lastname
```

where "lastname" is the last name of the person you're looking for.

6.7 When Things Go Wrong

• Nothing happens when you try to connect to a telnet site.
  The site could be down for maintenance or problems.

• You get a "host unavailable" message.
  The telnet site is down for some reason. Try again later.

• You get a "host unknown" message.
  Check your spelling of the site name.

• You type in a password on a telnet site that requires one, and you get a "login incorrect" message.

  Try logging in again. If you get the message again, hit your control and] keys at the same time to disengage and return to your host system.

• You can't seem to disconnect from a telnet site.

  Use control-] to disengage and return to your host system.

6.8 FYI

The Usenet newsgroups alt.internet.services and alt.bbs.internet can provide pointers to new telnet systems. Scott Yanoff periodically posts his "Updated Internet Services List" in the former. The alt.bbs.internet newsgroup is also where you'll find Aydin Edguer's compendium of FAQs related to Internet bulletin board systems.

Peter Scott, who maintains the Hytelnet database, runs a mailing list about new telnet services and changes in existing ones. To get on the list, send him a note at scott@sklib.usask.ca.

Gleason Sackman maintains another mailing list dedicated to new Internet services and news about the new uses to which the Net is being put. To subscribe, send a message to listserv@internic.net. Leave the "subject:" line blank, and as your message, write: Sub net-happenings Your Name.

7 FTP

7.1 Tons of Files

Hundreds of systems connected to Internet have file libraries, or archives, accessible to the public. Much of this consists of free or low-cost shareware programs for virtually every make of computer. If you want a different communications program for your IBM, or feel like playing a new game on your Amiga, you'll be able to get it from the Net.

But there are also libraries of documents as well. If you want a copy of a recent U.S. Supreme Court decision, you can find it on the Net. Copies of historical documents, from the Magna Carta to the Declaration of Independence, are also yours for the asking, along with a translation of a telegram from Lenin ordering the execution of rebellious peasants. You can also find song lyrics, poems, even summaries of every *Lost in Space* episode ever made. You can also find extensive files detailing everything you could ever possibly want to know about the Net itself. First you'll see how to get these files, then we'll show you where they're kept.

The most common way to get these files is through the file transfer protocol, or ftp. As with telnet, not all systems that connect to the Net have access to ftp. However, if your system is one of these, you'll be able to get many of these files through e-mail (see the next chapter).

Starting ftp is as easy as using telnet. At your host system's command line, type

```
ftp site.name
```

and hit enter, where "site.name" is the address of the ftp site you want to reach. One major difference between telnet and ftp is that it is considered bad form to connect to most ftp sites during their business hours (generally 6 A.M. to 6 P.M. local time). This is because transferring files across the network takes up considerable computing power, which during the day is likely to be needed for whatever the computer's main function is. There are some ftp sites that are accessible to the public 24 hours a day, though. You'll find these noted in the list of ftp sites in section 7.6.

7.2 Your Friend Archie

How do you find a file you want, though?

Until a few years ago, this could be quite the pain—there was no master directory to tell you where a given file might be stored on the Net. Who'd want to slog through hundreds of file libraries looking for something?

Alan Emtage, Bill Heelan, and Peter Deutsch, students at McGill University in Montreal, asked the same question. Unlike the weather, though, they did something about it.

They created a database system, called archie, that would periodically call up file libraries and basically find out what they had available. In turn, anybody could dial into archie, type in a file name, and see where on the Net it was available. Archie currently catalogs close to a thousand file libraries around the world.

Today, there are three ways to ask archie to find a file for you: through telnet, a "client" archie program on your own host system, or e-mail. All three methods let you type in a full or partial file name and will tell you where on the Net it's stored. If you have access to telnet, you can telnet to one of the following addresses: archie.mcgill.ca, archie.sura.net, archie.unl.edu, archie.ans.net, or archie.rutgers.edu. If asked for a log-in name, type

```
archie
```

and hit enter.

When you connect, the key command is prog, which you use in this form:

```
prog filename
```

followed by enter, where "filename" is the program or file you're looking for. If you're unsure of a file's complete name, try typing part of the name. For example, "PKZIP" will work as well as "PKZIP204.EXE." The system does not support DOS or Unix wildcards. If you ask archie to look for "PKZIP*," it will tell you it couldn't find anything by that name. One thing to keep in mind is that a file is not necessarily the same as a program—it could also be a document. This means you can use archie to search for, say, everything online related to the Beatles, as well as computer programs and graphics files.

A number of Net sites now have their own archie programs that take your request for information and pass it onto the nearest archie database—ask your system administrator if your system has it online. These "client" programs seem to provide information a lot more quickly than the actual archie itself! If it is available, at your host system's command line, type

```
archie -s filename
```

where filename is the program or document you're looking for, and hit enter. The -s tells the program to ignore case in a file name and lets you search for partial matches. You might actually want to type it this way:

```
archie -s filename|more
```

which will stop the output every screen (handy if there are many sites that carry the file you want). Or you could open a file on your computer with your text-logging function.

The third way, for people without access to either of the previous ways, is e-mail.

Send a message to archie@quiche.cs.mcgill.ca. You can leave the subject line blank. Inside the message, type

```
prog filename
```

where filename is the file you're looking for. You can ask archie to look up several programs by putting their names on the same "prog" line, like this:

```
prog file1 file2 file3
```

Within a few hours, archie will write back with a list of the appropriate sites.

In all three cases, if there is a system that has your file, you'll get a response that looks something like this:

```
Host sumex-aim.stanford.edu

Location: /info-mac/comm
    FILE -rw-r--r--   258256   Feb 15 17:07   zterm-09.hqx
```

```
Location: /info-mac/misc
  FILE -rw-r—r—@PARA = 7490 Sep 12 1991 zterm-sys7-color-
icons.hqx
```

Chances are, you will get a number of similar-looking responses for each program. The "host" is the system that has the file. The "location" tells you which directory to look in when you connect to that system. Ignore the funny-looking collections of r's and hyphens for now. After them, come the size of the file or directory listing in bytes, the date it was uploaded, and the name of the file.

7.3 Getting the Files

Now you want to get that file.

Assuming your host site does have ftp, you connect in a similar fashion to telnet, by typing

```
ftp sumex-aim.stanford.edu
```

(or the name of whichever site you want to reach). Hit enter. If the connection works, you'll see this:

```
Connected to sumex-aim.stanford.edu.
220 SUMEX-AIM FTP server (Version 4.196 Mon Jan 13
13:52:23 PST 1992) ready.
Name (sumex-aim.stanford.edu:adamg):
```

If nothing happens after a minute or so, hit control-C to return to your host system's command line. But if it has worked, type

```
anonymous
```

and hit enter. You'll see a lot of references on the Net to "anonymous ftp." This is how it gets its name—you don't really have to tell the library site what your name is. The reason is that these sites are set up so that anybody can gain access to certain public files, while letting people with accounts on the sites to log on and access their own personal files. Next, you'll be asked for your password. As a password, use your e-mail address. This will then come up:

```
230 Guest connection accepted. Restrictions apply.
Remote system type is UNIX.
Using binary mode to transfer files.
ftp>
```

Now type

```
ls
```

and hit enter. You'll see something awful like this:

```
200 PORT command successful.
150 Opening ASCII mode data connection for /bin/ls.
total 2636
-rw-rw-r-- 1 0      31     4444 Mar  3 11:34 README.POSTING
dr-xr-xr-x 2 0      1       512 Nov  8 11:06 bin
-rw-r--r-- 1 0      0 11030960 Apr  2 14:06 core
dr--r--r-- 2 0      1       512 Nov  8 11:06 etc
drwxrwsr-x 5 13     22      512 Mar 19 12:27 imap
drwxr-xr-x 25 1016  31      512 Apr  4 02:15 info-mac
drwxr--- 2 0        31     1024 Apr  5 15:38 pid
drwxrwsr-x 13 0     20     1024 Mar 27 14:03 pub
drwxr-xr-x 2 1077   20      512 Feb  6 1989 tmycin
226 Transfer complete.
ftp>
```

Ack! Let's decipher this Rosetta stone.

First, ls is the ftp command for displaying a directory (you can actually use dir as well, but if you're used to MS-DOS, this could lead to confusion when you try to use dir on your host system, where it won't work, so it's probably better to just remember to always use ls for a directory while online).

The very first letter on each line tells you whether the listing is for a directory or a file. If the first letter is a d or an l, it's a directory. Otherwise, it's a file.

The rest of that weird set of letters and dashes consists of "flags" that tell the ftp site who can look at, change, or delete the file. You can safely ignore it. You can also ignore the rest of the line until you get to the second number, the one just before the date. This tells you how large the file is, in bytes. If the line is for a directory, the number gives you a rough indication of how many items are in that directory—a directory listing of 512 bytes is relatively small. Next comes the date the file or directory was uploaded, followed (finally!) by its name.

Notice the README.POSTING file up at the top of the directory. Most archive sites have a "read me" document, which usually contains some basic information about the site, its resources, and how to use them. Let's get this file, both for the information in it and to see how to transfer files from there to here. At the ftp> prompt, type

```
get README                    '
```

and hit enter. Note that ftp sites are no different from Unix sites in general: they are case sensitive. You'll see something like this:

```
200 PORT command successful.
150 Opening BINARY mode data connection for README (4444
bytes).
226 Transfer complete. 4444 bytes received in 1.177sec-
onds (3.8 Kbytes/s)
```

And that's it! The file is now located in your home directory on your host system, from which you can now download it to your own computer. The simple "get" command is the key to transferring a file from an archive site to your host system.

If you want to download more than one file at a time (say a series of documents), use mget instead of get; for example:

```
mget *.txt
```

This will transfer copies of every file ending with .txt in the given directory. Before each file is copied, you'll be asked if you're sure you want it. Despite this, mget could still save you considerable time—you won't have to type in every single file name. If you want to save even more time, and are sure you really want ALL of the given files, type

```
prompt
```

before you do the mget command. This will turn off the prompt, and all the files will be zapped right into your home directory.

There is one other command to keep in mind. If you want to get a copy of a computer program, type

```
bin
```

and hit enter. This tells the ftp site and your host site that you are sending a binary file, that is, a program. Most ftp sites now use binary format as a default, but it's a good idea to do this in case you've connected to one of the few that doesn't.

To switch to a directory, type

```
cd directory-name
```

(substituting the name of the directory you want to access) and hit enter. Type

```
ls
```

and hit enter to get the file listing for that particular directory. To move back up the directory tree, type

```
cd ..
```

(note the space between the d and the first period) and hit enter. Or you could type

```
cdup
```

and hit enter. Keep doing this until you get to the directory of interest. Alternately, if you already know the directory path of the file you want (from our friend archie), after you connect, you could simply type this:

```
get directory/subdirectory/filename
```

On many sites, files meant for public consumption are in the pub or public directory; sometimes you'll see an info directory.

Almost every site has a bin directory, which at first glance sounds like a bin in which interesting stuff might be dumped. But it actually stands for "binary" and is simply a place for the system administrator to store the programs that run the ftp system. Lost+found is another directory that looks interesting but actually never has anything of public interest in it.

Before, you saw how to use archie. From our example, you can see that some system administrators go a little berserk when naming files. Fortunately, there's a way for you to rename the file as it's being transferred. Using our archie example, you'd type

```
get zterm-sys7-color-icons.hqx zterm.hqx
```

and hit enter. Instead of having to deal constantly with a file called zterm-sys7-color-icons.hqx, you'll now have one called, simply, zterm.hqx.

Those last three letters bring up something else: Many program files are compressed to save on space and transmission time. In order to actually use them, you'll have to use an uncompress program on them first.

7.4 Odd Letters—Decoding File Endings

There is a wide variety of compression methods in use. You can tell which method was used by the last one to three letters at the end of a file. Here are some of the more common ones and what you'll need to uncompress the files they create (most of these decompression programs can be located through archie).

.txt or .TXT	By itself, this means the file is a document, rather than a program.
.ps or .PS	A PostScript document (in Adobe's page description language). You can print this file on any PostScript-capable printer
.doc or .DOC	Another common "extension" for documents. No decompression is needed
.Z	This indicates a Unix compression method. To uncompress

```
uncompress filename.Z
```

and hit enter at your host system's command line. If the file is a compressed text file

```
zcat filename.txt.Z |more
```

u16.zip is an MS-DOS program that will let you download such a file and uncompress it on your own computer. The Macintosh equivalent program is called MacCompress (use archie to find these).

.zip or .ZIP	These indicate the file has been compressed with a common MS-DOS compression program
.gz	A Unix version of ZIP. To uncompress

```
gunzip filename.gz
```

at your host system's command line.

.zoo or .ZOO	A Unix and MS-DOS compression format. Use a program called zoo to uncompress.
.Hqx or .hqx	Macintosh compression format. Requires the BinHex program.
.shar or .Shar	Another Unix format. Use unshar to uncompress.
.tar	Another Unix format

.sit or .Sit	A Macintosh format that requires the Stuffit program.
.ARC	Another MS-DOS format
.LHZ	Another MS-DOS format; requires the use of LHARC.

A few last words of caution: Check the size of a file before you get it. The Net moves data at phenomenal rates of speed. But that 500,000-byte file that gets transferred to your host system in a few seconds could take more than an hour or two to download to your computer if you're using a 2400-baud modem. Your host system may also have limits on the amount of bytes you can store online at any one time. Also, although it is really extremely unlikely you will ever get a file infected with a virus, if you plan to do much downloading over the Net, you'd be wise to invest in a good antiviral program, just in case.

7.5 The Keyboard Cabal

System administrators are like everybody else—they try to make things easier for themselves. And when you sit in front of a keyboard all day, that can mean trying everything possible to reduce the number of keys you actually have to hit each day.

Unfortunately, that can make it difficult for the rest of us.

You've already read about bin and lost+found directories. Etc is another seemingly interesting directory that turns out to be another place to store files used by the ftp site itself. Again, nothing of any real interest.

Then, once you get into the actual file libraries, you'll find that in many cases, files will have such nondescriptive names as V1.1-AK.TXT. The best-known example is probably a set of several hundred files known as RFCs, which provide the basic technical and organizational information on which much of the Internet is built. These files can be found on many ftp sites, but always in a form such as RFC101.TXT, RFC102.TXT and so on, with no clue whatsoever as to what information they contain.

Fortunately, almost all ftp sites have a Rosetta stone to help you decipher these names. Most will have a file named README (or some variant) that gives basic information about the system. Then, most directories will either have a similar README file or will have an index that does give brief descriptions of each file. These are usually the first file in a directory and often are in the form 00INDEX.TXT. Use the get command to get this file. You can then scan it online or download it to see which files you might be interested in.

Another file you will frequently see is called ls-lR.Z. This contains a listing of every file on the system, but without any descriptions (the name comes from the Unix command ls -lR, which gives you a listing of all the files in all your directories). The Z at the end means the file has been compressed, which means you will have to use a Unix uncompress command before you can read the file.

And finally, we have those system administrators who almost seem to delight in making things difficult—the ones who take full advantage of Unix's ability to create absurdly long file names. On some FTP sites, you will see file names as long as 80 characters or so, full of capital letters, underscores, and every other orthographic device that will make it almost impossible for you to type the file name correctly when you try to get it. Your secret weapon here is the mget command. Just type mget, a space, and the first five or six letters of the file name, followed by an asterisk. For example:

```
mget This_F*
```

The FTP site will ask you if you want to get the file that begins with that name. If there are several files that start that way, you might have to answer 'n' a few times, but it's still easier than trying to re-create a ludicrously long file name.

7.6 Some Interesting FTP Sites

What follows is a list of some interesting ftp sites, arranged by category. With hundreds of ftp sites now on the Net, however, this list barely scratches the surface of what is available. Liberal use of archie will help you find specific files.

The times listed for each site are in eastern time and represent the periods during which it is considered acceptable to connect.

Amiga

ftp.uu.net Has Amiga programs in the systems/amiga directory. Available 24 hours.

wuarchive.wustl.edu Look in the pub/aminet directory. Available 24 hours.

Atari

atari.archive.umich.edu Find almost all the Atari files you'll ever need, in the atari directory. 7 P.M.–7 A.M.

Books

rtfm.mit.edu The pub/usenet/rec.arts.books directory has reading lists for various authors as well as lists of recommended bookstores in different cities. Unfortunately, this site uses incredibly long file names—so long they may scroll off the end of your screen if you are using MS-DOS or certain other computers. Even if you want just one of the files, it probably makes more sense to use mget than get. This way, you will be asked on each file whether you want to get it; otherwise you may wind up frustrated because the system will keep telling you the file you want doesn't exist (since you may miss the end of its name due to the scrolling problem). 6 P.M.–6 A.M.

mrcnext.cso.uiuc.edu Project Gutenberg is an effort to translate paper texts into electronic form. Already available are more than a hundred titles, from works by authors from Lewis Carroll to Mark Twain; from *A Tale of Two Cities* to *Son of Tarzan*. Look in the /etext/etext92 and /etext/etext93 directories. 6 P.M.–9 A.M.

Computer Ethics

ftp.eff.org The home of the Electronic Frontier Foundation. Use cd to get to the pub directory and then look in the EFF, SJG, and CPSR directories for documents on the EFF itself and various issues related to the Net, ethics, and the law. Available 24 hours.

Consumer

rtfm.mit.edu The pub/usenet/misc.consumers directory has documents related to credit. The pub/usenet/rec.travel.air directory will tell you how to deal with airline reservation clerks, find the best prices on seats, etc. See Books for a caveat in using this ftp site. 6 P.M.–6 A.M.

Cooking

wuarchive.wustl.edu Look for recipes and recipe directories in the usenet/rec.food.cooking/recipes directory.

gatekeeper.dec.com Recipes are in the pub/recipes directory.

Economics

neeedc.umesbs.maine.edu (Yes, there are three "e"s in "neeedc.") The Federal Reserve Bank of Boston uses this site to house all sorts of data on the New England economy. Many files contain 20 years or more of information, usually in forms that are easily adaptable to spreadsheet or database files. Look in the frbb directory. 6 P.M.–6 A.M.

town.hall.org Look in the edgar directory for the beginnings of a system to distribute annual reports and other data publicly held companies are required to file with the Securities and Exchange Commission. The other/fed directory holds various statistical files from the Federal Reserve Board.

FTP

iraun1.ira.uka.de Run by the computer science department of the University of Karlsruhe in Germany, this site offers lists of anonymous FTP sites both internationally (in the anon.ftp.sites directory) and in Germany (in anon.ftp.sites.DE). Noon to 2 A.M.

ftp.netcom.com The pub/profiles directory has lists of ftp sites.

Government

ncsuvm.cc.ncsu.edu The SENATE directory contains bibliographic records of U.S. Senate hearings and documents for the past several Congresses. Get the file README.DOS9111, which will explain the cryptic file names. 6 P.M.–6 A.M.

nptn.org The General Accounting Office is the investigative wing of Congress. The pub/e.texts/gao.reports directory represents an experiment by the agency to use ftp to distribute its reports. Available 24 hours.

info.umd.edu The info/Government/US/Whitehouse directory has copies of press releases and other documents from the Clinton administration. 6 P.M.–6 A.M.

leginfo.public.ca.gov This is a repository of legislative calendars, bills and other information related to state government in California. Available 24 hours.

whitehouse.gov Look for copies of presidential position papers, transcripts of press conferences and related information here. Available 24 hours.

See also Law.

History

nptn.org This site has a large, growing collection of text files. In the pub/e.texts/freedom.shrine directory, you'll find copies of important historical documents, from the Magna Carta to the Declaration of Independence and the Emancipation Proclamation. Available 24 hours.

ra.msstate.edu Mississippi State maintains an eclectic database of historical documents, detailing everything from Attilla's battle strategy to songs of soldiers in Vietnam, in the docs/history directory. 6 P.M.–6 A.M.

seq1.loc.gov The Library of Congress has acquired numerous documents from the former Soviet government and has translated many of them into English. In the pub/soviet.archive/text.english directory, you'll find everything from telegrams from Lenin ordering the death of peasants to Khrushchev's response to Kennedy during the Cuban Missile Crisis. The README file in the pub/soviet.archive directory provides an index to the documents. 6 P.M.–6 A.M.

Hong Kong

nok.lcs.mit.edu GIF pictures of Hong Kong pop stars, buildings, and vistas are available in the pub/hongkong/HKPA directory. 6 P.M.–6 A.M.

Internet

ftp.eff.org The pub/Net_info directory has a number of subdirectories containing various Internet resources guides and information files, including the latest online version of *Everybody's Guide to the Internet*, entitled *EFF's Guide to the Internet*. Available 24 hours.

nic.ddn.mil The internet-drafts directory contains information about Internet, while the scc directory holds network security bulletins. 6 P.M.–6 A.M.

Law

info.umd.edu U.S. Supreme Court decisions from 1989 to the present are stored in the info/Government/US/SupremeCt directory. Each term has a separate directory (for example, term1992). Get the README and Index files to help decipher the case numbers. 6 P.M.–6 A.M.

ftp.uu.net Supreme Court decisions are in the court-opinions directory. You'll want to get the index file, which tells you which file numbers go with which file names. The decisions come in WordPerfect and Atex format only. Available 24 hours.

Libraries

ftp.unt.edu The library directory contains numerous lists of libraries with computerized card catalogs accessible through the Net.

Literature

nptn.org In the pub/e.texts/gutenberg/etext91 and etext92 directories, you can get copies of Aesop's *Fables*, works by Lewis Carroll, and other works of literature, as well as the Book of Mormon. Available 24 hours.

world.std.com The obi directory has everything from online fables to accounts of Hiroshima survivors. 6 P.M.–6 A.M.

Macintosh

sumex-aim.stanford.edu This is the premier site for Macintosh software. After you log in, switch to the info-mac directory, which will bring up a long series of subdirectories of virtually every free and shareware Mac program you could ever want. 9 P.M.–9 A.M.

ftp.uu.net You'll find lots of Macintosh programs in the systems/mac/simtel20 directory. Available 24 hours.

Movie Reviews

lcs.mit.edu Look in the movie-reviews directory. 6 P.M.–6 A.M.

MS-DOS

wuarchive.wustl.edu This carries one of the world's largest collections of MS-DOS software. The files are actually copied, or "mirrored," from a computer at the U.S. Army's White Sands Missile Range. It also carries large collections of Macintosh, Windows, Atari, Amiga, Unix, OS9, CP/M, and Apple II software. Look in the mirrors and systems directories. The gif directory contains a large number of GIF graphics images. Accessible 24 hours.

ftp.uu.net Look for MS-DOS programs and files in the systems/msdos/simtel20 directory. Available 24 hours.

Music

cs.uwp.edu The pub/music directory has everything from lyrics of contemporary songs to recommended CDs of baroque music. It's a little different—and easier to navigate—than other ftp sites. File and directory names are on the left, while on the right, you'll find a brief description of the file or directory, like this:

```
SITES1528 Other music-related FTP archive sitesclassical/
-(dir) Classical Buying Guide
database/- (dir) Music Database program
discog/= (dir) Discographies
faqs/= (dir) Music Frequently Asked questions files
folk/- (dir) Folk Music Files and pointers
guitar/= (dir) Guitar TAB files from ftp.nevada.eduinfo/
= (dir) rec.music.info archives
interviews/- (dir) Interviews with musicians/groups
lists/= (dir) Mailing lists archives
lyrics/= (dir) Lyrics Archives
misc/- (dir) Misc files that don't fit anywhere else
pictures/= (dir) GIFS, JPEGs, PBMs and more.
press/- (dir) Press Releases and misc articles
programs/- (dir) Misc music-related programs for various
machines
```

```
releases/= (dir) Upcoming USA release listing
sounds/= (dir) Short sound samples
226 Transfer complete.
ftp>
```

When you switch to a directory, don't include the /. 7 P.M.–7 A.M.

potemkin.cs.pdx.edu The Bob Dylan archive. Interviews, notes, year-by-year accounts of his life and more, in the pub/dylan directory. 9 P.M.–9 A.M.

ftp.nevada.edu Guitar chords for contemporary songs are in the pub/guitar directory, in subdirectories organized by group or artist.

Native Americans

pines.hsu.edu Home of IndianNet, this site contains a variety of directories and files related to Indians and Eskimos, including federal census data, research reports, and a tribal profiles database. Look in the pub and indian directories.

Pets

rtfm.mit.edu The pub/usenet/rec.pets.dogs and pub/usenet.rec.-pets.cats directories have documents on the respective animals. See Books for a caveat in using this ftp site. 6 P.M.–6 A.M.

Photography

ftp.nevada.edu Photolog is an online digest of photography news, in the pub/photo directory.

Pictures

wuarchive.wustl.edu The graphics/gif directory contains hundreds of GIF photographic and drawing images, from cartoons to cars, space images to pop stars. These are arranged in a long series of subdirectories.

Religion

nptn.org In the pub/e.texts/religion directory, you'll find subdirectories for chapters and books of both the Bible and the Koran. Available 24 hours.

Science Fiction

elbereth.rutgers.edu In the pub/sfl directory, you'll find plot summaries for various science-fiction TV shows, including *Star Trek* (not only the original and Next Generation shows, but the cartoon version as well), *Lost in Space, Battlestar Galactica, The Twilight Zone, The Prisoner,* and *Doctor Who.* There are also lists of various things related to science fiction and an online science fiction fanzine. 6 P.M.–6 A.M.

Sex

rtfm.mit.edu Look in the pub/usenet/alt.sex and pub/usenet/alt.sex.wizards directories for documents related to all facets of sex. See Books for a caveat in using this ftp site. 6 P.M.–6 A.M.

Shakespeare

atari.archive.umich.edu The shakespeare directory contains most of the Bard's works. A number of other sites have his works as well, but generally as one huge megafile. This site breaks them down into various categories (comedies, poetry, histories, etc.) so that you can download individual plays or sonnets.

Space

ames.arc.nasa.gov Stores text files about space and the history of the NASA space program in the pub/SPACE subdirectory. In the pub/GIF and pub/SPACE/GIF directories, you'll find astronomy- and NASA-related GIF files, including pictures of planets, satellites, and other celestial objects. 9 P.M.–9 A.M.

Travel

nic.stolaf.edu Before you take that next overseas trip, you might want to see whether the State Department has issued any kind of advisory for the countries on your itinerary. The advisories, which cover everything from hurricane damage to civil war, are in the pub/travel-advisories/advisories directory, arranged by country. 7 P.M.–7 A.M.

TV

coe.montana.edu The pub/TV/Guides directory has histories and other information about dozens of TV shows. Only two anonymous-ftp log-ins are allowed at a time, so you might have to try more than once to get in. 8 P.M.–8 A.M.

ftp.cs.widener.edu The pub/simpsons directory has more files than anybody could possibly need about Bart and family. The pub/strek directory has files about the original and Next Generation shows as well as the movies.

See also Science Fiction.

Usenet

ftp.uu.net In the usenet directory, you'll find "frequently asked questions" files, copied from rtfm.mit.edu. The communications directory holds programs that let MS-DOS users connect directly with UUCP sites. In the info directory, you'll find information about ftp and ftp sites. The inet directory contains information about Internet. Available 24 hours.

rtfm.mit.edu This site contains all available "frequently asked questions" files for Usenet newsgroups in the pub/usenet directory. See Books for a caveat in using this ftp site. 6 P.M.–6 A.M.

Viruses

ftp.unt.edu The antivirus directory has antivirus programs for MS-DOS and Macintosh computers. 7 P.M.–7 A.M.

Weather

wuarchive.wustl.edu The /multimedia/images/wx directory contains GIF weather images of North America. Files are updated hourly
and take this general form: CV100222. The first two letters tell the type
of file: CV means it is a visible-light photo taken by a weather satellite.
CI images are similar, but use infrared light. Both these are in black
and white. Files that begin with SA are color radar maps of the United
States that show severe weather patterns but also fronts and tempera-
tures in major cities. The numbers indicate the date and time (in
GMT—five hours ahead of EST) of the image: the first two numbers
represent the month, the next two the date, the last two the hour. The
file WXKEY.GIF explains the various symbols in SA files.

7.7 ncftp—Now You Tell Me!

If you're lucky, the people who run your host system or public-access
site have installed a program called ncftp, which takes some of the
edges off the ftp process.

For starters, when you use ncftp instead of plain old ftp, you no
longer have to worry about misspelling "anonymous" when you connect. The program does it for you. And once you're in, instead of
getting line after line filled with dashes, x's, r's, and d's, you only get
listings of the files or directories themselves (if you're used to MS-DOS,
the display you get will be very similar to that produced by the
dir/w command). The program even creates a list of the ftp sites
you've used most recently, so you can pick from that list, instead of
trying to remember some incredibly complex ftp site name.

Launching the program, assuming your site has it, is easy. At the
command prompt, type

```
ncftp sitename
```

where "sitename" is the site you want to reach (alternately, you could
type just ncftp and then use its open command). Once connected, you
can use the same ftp commands you've become used to, such as ls,
get, and mget. Entries that end in a / are directories to which you can
switch with cd; others are files you can get. A couple of useful ncftp
commands include type, which lets you change the type of file transfer
(from ASCII to binary, for example) and size, which lets you see how
large a file is before you get it. For example,

```
size declaration.txt
```

would tell you how large the declaration.txt file is before you get it. When you say "bye" to disconnect from a site, ncftp remembers the last directory you were in, so that the next time you connect to the site, you are put back into that directory automatically. If you type

```
help
```

you'll get a list of files you can read to extend the power of the program even further.

7.8 Project Gutenberg—Electronic Books

Project Gutenberg, coordinated by Michael Hart, has a fairly ambitious goal: to make more than ten thousand books and other documents available electronically by the year 2001. In 1993, the project uploaded an average of four books a month to its ftp sites; in 1994, they hope to double the pace.

Begun in 1971, the project already maintains a "library" of hundreds of books and stories, from Aesop's *Fables* to *Through the Looking Glass*, available for the taking. It also has a growing number of current-affairs documents, such as the CIA's annual *World Factbook* almanac.

Besides nptn.org, Project Gutenberg texts can be retrieved from mrcnext.cso.uiuc.edu in the etext directory.

7.9 When Things Go Wrong

- You get a "host unavailable" message.
  The ftp site is down for some reason. Try again later.
- You get a "host unknown" message.
  Check your spelling of the site name.

• You misspell "anonymous" when logging in and get a message telling you a password is required for whatever you typed in.

Type something in, hit enter, type bye, hit enter, and try again. Alternately, try typing ftp instead of anonymous. It will work on a surprising number of sites. Or just use ncftp, if your site has it, and never worry about this again.

7.10 FYI

Liberal use of archie will help you find specific files or documents. For information on new or interesting ftp sites, try the comp.archives newsgroup on Usenet. You can also look in the comp.misc, comp.sources.wanted, or news.answers newsgroups on Usenet for lists of ftp sites posted every month by Tom Czarnik and Jon Granrose.

The comp.archives newsgroup carries news of new ftp sites and interesting new files on existing sites.

In the comp.virus newsgroup on Usenet, look for postings that list ftp sites carrying antiviral software for Amiga, MS-DOS, Macintosh, Atari, and other computers.

The comp.sys.ibm.pc.digest and comp.sys.mac.digest newsgroups provide information about new MS-DOS and Macintosh programs as well as answers to questions from users of those computers.

8

Gophers, WAISs, and the World-Wide Web

8.1 Gophers

Even with tools like Hytelnet and archie, telnet and ftp can still be frustrating. There are all those telnet and ftp addresses to remember. Telnet services often have their own unique commands. And, oh, those weird directory and file names!

But now that the Net has become a rich repository of information, people are developing ways to make it far easier to find and retrieve information and files. Gophers and Wide-Area Information Servers (WAISs) are two services that could ultimately make the Internet as easy to navigate as commercial networks such as CompuServe or Prodigy.

Both gophers and WAISs essentially take a request for information and then scan the Net for it, so you don't have to. Both also work through menus—instead of typing in some long sequence of characters, you just move a cursor to your choice and hit enter. Gophers even let you select files and programs from ftp sites this way.

Let's first look at gophers (named for the official mascot of the University of Minnesota, where the system was developed).

Many public-access sites now have gophers online. To use one, type

```
gopher
```

at the command prompt and hit enter. If you know your site does not have a gopher, or if nothing happens when you type that, telnet to the following address:

```
consultant.micro.umn.edu
```

At the log-in prompt, type

```
gopher
```

and hit enter. You'll be asked what type of terminal emulation you're using, after which you'll see something like this:

```
Internet Gopher Information Client v1.03

Root gopher server: gopher.micro.umn.edu

-->   1. Information About Gopher/
      2. Computer Information/
      3. Discussion Groups/
      4. Fun & Games/
      5. Internet file server (ftp) sites/
      6. Libraries/
      7. News/
      8. Other Gopher and Information Servers/
      9. Phone Books/
      10. Search lots of places at the U of M <?>
      11. University of Minnesota Campus Information/

Press ? for Help, q to Quit, u to go up a menu  Page: 1/1
```

Assuming you're using VT100 or some other VT emulation, you'll be able to move among the choices with your up- and down-arrow keys. When you have your cursor on an entry that looks interesting, just hit enter, and you'll either get a new menu of choices, a database entry form, or a text file, depending on what the menu entry is linked to (more on how to tell which you'll get in a moment).

Gophers are great for exploring the resources of the Net. Just keep making choices to see what pops up. Play with it; see where it takes you. Some choices will be documents. When you read one of these and either come to the end or hit a lowercase q to quit reading it, you'll be given the choice of saving a copy to your home directory or e-mailing it to yourself. Other choices are simple databases that let you enter a word to look for in a particular database. To get back to where you started on a gopher, hit your u key at a menu prompt, which will move you back "up" through the gopher menu structure (much like "cd .." in ftp).

Notice that one of your choices is "Internet file server (ftp) sites." Choose this, and you'll be connected to a modified archie program—an archie with a difference. When you search for a file through a gopher archie, you'll get a menu of sites that have the file you're looking for, just as with the old archie. Only now, instead of having to write down or remember an ftp address and directory, all you have to do is position the cursor next to one of the numbers in the menu and hit enter. You'll be connected to the ftp site, from which you can then choose the file you want. This time, move the cursor to the file you want and hit a lowercase s. You'll be asked for a name in your home directory to use for the file, after which the file will be copied to your home system. Unfortunately, this file transfer process does not yet work with all public-access sites for computer programs and compressed files. If it doesn't work with yours, you'll have to get the file the old-fashioned way, via anonymous ftp.

In addition to ftp sites, there are hundreds of databases and libraries around the world accessible through gophers. There is not yet a common gopher interface for library catalogs, so be prepared to follow the online directions more closely when you use gopher to connect to one.

Gopher menu entries that end in a / are gateways to another menu of options. Entries that end in a period are text, graphics, or program files, which you can retrieve to your home directory (or e-mail to yourself or to somebody else). A line that ends in <?> or <CSO> represents a request you can make to a database for information. The difference is that <?> entries call up one-line interfaces in which you can search for a keyword or words, while <CSO> brings up an electronic form with several fields for you to fill out (you might see this in online "White Pages" directories at colleges).

Gophers actually let you perform some relatively sophisticated Boolean searches. For example, if you want to search only for files that contain the words "MS-DOS" and "Macintosh," you'd type

```
ms-dos and macintosh
```

(gophers are not case sensitive) in the keyword field. Alternately, if you want to get a list of files that mention either "MS-DOS" or "Macintosh," you'd type

```
ms-dos or macintosh
```

8.2 Burrowing Deeper

As fascinating as it can be to explore "gopherspace," you might one day want to retrieve some information, or a file, quickly. Or you might grow tired of calling up endless menus to get to the one you want. Fortunately, there are ways to make even gophers easier to use.

One is with archie's friend, veronica (it allegedly is an acronym, but don't believe that for a second), who does for gopherspace what archie does for ftp sites.

In most gophers, you'll find veronica by selecting "Other gopher and information services" at the main menu and then "Searching through gopherspace using veronica." You'll get something like this:

```
Internet Gopher Information Client v1.1

Search titles in Gopherspace using veronica

-->   1.
      2. FAQ: Frequently-Asked Questions about veronica
         (1993/08/23).
      3. How to compose veronica queries (NEW June 24)
         READ ME!!.
      4. Search Gopher Directory Titles at PSINet <?>
      5. Search Gopher Directory Titles at SUNET <?>
      6. Search Gopher Directory Titles at U. of Manitoba
         <?>
      7. Search Gopher Directory Titles at University of
         Cologne <?>
      8. Search gopherspace at PSINet <?>
      9. Search gopherspace at SUNET <?>
      10. Search gopherspace at U. of Manitoba <?>
      11. Search gopherspace at University of Cologne <?>

Press ? for Help, q to Quit, u to go up a menu   Page: 1/1
```

A few choices there! First, the difference between searching directory titles and just plain ol' gopherspace. If you already know the sort of directory you're looking for (say a directory containing MS-DOS programs), do a directory-title search. But if you're not sure what kind of directory your information might be in, then do a general gopherspace search. In general, it doesn't matter which of the particular veronicas you use—they should all be able to produce the same results. The reason there is more than one is because the Internet has become so popular that only one veronica (or one gopher or one of almost anything) would quickly be overwhelmed by all the information requests from around the world.

You can use veronica to search for almost anything. Want to find museums that might have online displays from their exhibits? Try searching for "museum." Looking for a copy of the Declaration of Independence? Try "declaration."

In many cases, your search will bring up a new gopher menu of choices to try.

Say you want to impress those guests coming over for dinner on Friday by cooking cherries flambé. If you were to call up veronica and type in "flambé" after calling up veronica, you would soon get a menu listing several flambé recipes, including one called "dessert flambé." Put your cursor on that line of the menu and hit enter, and you'll find it's a menu for cherries flambé. Then hit your q key to quit, and gopher will ask you if you want to save the file in your home directory on your public-access site or whether you want to e-mail it somewhere.

As you can see, you can use veronica as an alternative to archie, which, because of the Internet's growing popularity, seems to take longer and longer to work.

In addition to archie and veronica, we now also have jugheads (no bettys yet, though). These work the same as veronicas, but their searches are limited to the specific gopher systems on which they reside.

If there are particular gopher resources you use frequently, there are a couple of ways to get to them even more directly.

One is to use gopher in a manner similar to the way you can use telnet. If you know a particular gopher's Internet address (often the same as its telnet or ftp address), you can connect to it directly, rather than going through menus. For example, say you want to use the gopher at info.umd.edu. If your public-access site has a gopher system installed, type

```
gopher info.umd.edu
```

at your command prompt, and you'll be connected.

But even that can get tedious if there are several gophers you use frequently. That's where bookmarks come in. Gophers let you create a list of your favorite gopher sites and even database queries. Then, instead of digging ever deeper into the gopher directory structure, you just call up your bookmark list and select the service you want.

To create a bookmark for a particular gopher site, first call up gopher. Then go through all the gopher menus until you get to the menu you want. Type a capital A. You'll be given a suggested name for the bookmark entry, which you can change if you want by back-spacing over the suggestion and typing in your own. When done, hit enter. Now, whenever you're in gopherspace and want to zip back to that particular gopher service, just hit your V key (upper- or lowercase; in this instance, gopher doesn't care) anywhere within gopher. This will bring up a list of your bookmarks. Move to the one you want and hit enter, and you'll be connected.

Using a capital A is also good for saving particular database or veronica queries that you use frequently (for example, searching for news stories on a particular topic if your public-access site maintains an indexed archive of wire-service news).

Instead of a capital A, you can also hit a lowercase a. This will bring you to the particular line within a menu, rather than show you the entire menu.

If you ever want to delete a bookmark, hit V within gopher, select the item you want to get rid of, and then hit your D key.

One more hint:

If you want to find the address of a particular gopher service, hit your = key after you've highlighted its entry in a gopher menu. You'll get back a couple of lines, most of which will be technicalese of no immediate value to most folks, but some of which will consist of the site's address.

8.3 Gopher Commands

a   Add a line in a gopher menu to your bookmark list.

A   Add an entire gopher menu or a database query to your bookmark list.

d   Delete an entry from your bookmark list (you have to hit v first).

q   Quit, or exit, a gopher. You'll be asked if you really want to.

Q   Quit, or exit, a gopher without being asked if you're sure.

s   Save a highlighted file to your home directory.

u   Move back up a gopher menu structure.

v   View your bookmark list.

=   Get information on the originating site of a gopher entry.

>   Move ahead one screen in a gopher menu.

<   Move back one screen in a gopher menu.

8.4 Some Interesting Gophers

There are now hundreds of gopher sites around the world. What follows is a list of some of them. Assuming your site has a gopher "client" installed, you can reach them by typing

```
gopher sitename
```

at your command prompt. Can't find what you're looking for? Remember to use veronica to look up categories and topics!

Agriculture

cyfer.esusda.gov	More agricultural statistics and regulations than most people will ever need.
usda.mannlib.cornell.edu	More than 140 different types of agricultural data, most in Lotus 1–2–3 spreadsheet format.

Animals

saimiri.primate.wisc.edu	Information on primates and animal-welfare laws.

Architecture

libra.arch.umich.edu	Maintains online exhibits of a variety of architectural images.

Art

marvel.loc.gov	The Library of Congress runs several online "galleries" of images from exhibits at the library. Many of these pictures, in GIF or JPEG format, are HUGE, so be careful what you get first. Exhibits include works of art from the Vatican, copies

of once-secret Soviet documents, and pictures of artifacts related to Columbus's 1492 voyage. At the main menu, select 2, then "Exhibits."

galaxy.ucr.edu

The California Museum of Photography maintains its own online galery here. At the main menu, select "Campus Events," then "California Museum of Photography," then "Network Exhibitions."

Astronomy

cast0.ast.cam.ac.uk

A gopher devoted to astronomy, run by the Institute of Astronomy and the Royal Greenwich Observatory, Cambridge, England.

Census

bigcat.missouri.edu

You'll find detailed federal census data for communities of more than ten thousand people, as well as for states and counties here. At the main menu, select "Reference and Information Center," then "United States and Missouri Census Information" and "United States Census."

Computers

wuarchive.wustl.edu

Dozens of directories with software for all sorts of computers. Most programs have to be "uncompressed" before you can use them.

sumex-aim.stanford.edu

A similar type of system, with the emphasis on Macintosh programs and files.

Disability

val-dor.cc.buffalo.edu   The Cornucopia of Disability Information carries numerous information resources on disability issues and links to other disability-related services.

Environment

ecosys.drdr.virginia.edu   Copies of Environmental Protection Agency factsheets on hundreds of chemicals, searchable by keyword. Select "Education" and then "Environmental fact sheets."

envirolink.org   Dozens of documents and files related to environmental activism around the world.

Entomology

spider.ento.csiro.au   All about creepy-crawly things, both the good and the bad ones.

Geology

gopher.stolaf.edu   Select "Internet Resources" and then "Weather and geography" for information on recent earthquakes.

Government

marvel.loc.gov   Run by the Library of Congress, this site provides numerous resources, including access to the Library card catalog and all manner of information about the U.S. Congress.

gopher.lib.umich.edu	Wide variety of government information, from Congressional committee assignments to economic statistics and NAFTA information.
ecix.doc.gov	Information on conversion of military installations to private uses.
sunsite.unc.edu	Copies of current and past federal budgets can be found by selecting "Sunsite archives," then "Politics," then "Sunsite politcal science archives."
wiretap.spies.com	Documents related to the Canadian government can be found in the "Government docs" menu.
stis.nih.gov	Select the "Other U.S. government gopher servers" for access to numerous other federal gophers.

Health

odie.niaid.nih.gov	National Institutes of Health databases on AIDS, in the "AIDS related information" menu.
helix.nih.gov	For National Cancer Institute factsheets on different cancers, select "Health and clinical information" and then "Cancernet information."
nysernet.org	Look for information on breast cancer in the "Special Collections: Breast Cancer" menu.
welchlink.welch.jhu.edu	This is Johns Hopkins University's medical gopher.

History

See Art.

Internet

gopher.lib.umich.edu

Home to several guides to Internet resources in specific fields, for example, social sciences. Select "What's New & Featured Resources" and then "Clearing-house."

Israel

jerusalem1.datasrv.co.il

This Israeli system offers numerous documents on Israel and Jewish life.

Japan

gopher.ncc.go.jp

Look in the "Japan information" menu for documents related to Japanese life and culture.

Music

mtv.com

Run by Adam Curry, an MTV video jock, this site has music news and Curry's daily "Cybersleaze" celebrity report.

Nature

ucmp1.berkeley.edu

The University of California at Berkeley's Museum of Paleontology runs several online exhibits here. You can obtain GIF images of plants and animals from the "Remote Nature" menu. The "Origin of the Species" menu lets you read Darwin's work or search it by keyword.

Sports

culine.colorado.edu   Look up schedules for teams in various professional sports leagues here, under "Professional Sports Schedules."

Weather

wx.atmos.uiuc.edu   Look up weather forecasts for North America or bone up on your weather facts.

8.5 Wide-Area Information Servers

Now you know there are hundreds of databases and library catalogs you can search through. But as you look, you begin to realize that each seems to have its own unique method for searching. If you connect to several, this can become a pain. Gophers reduce this problem somewhat.

Wide-area information servers promise another way to zero in on information hidden on the Net. In a WAIS, the user sees only one interface—the program worries about how to access information on dozens, even hundreds, of different databases. You give a WAIS a word and it scours the net looking for places where it's mentioned. You get a menu of documents, each ranked according to how relevant to your search the WAIS thinks it is.

Like gophers, WAIS "client" programs can already be found on many public-access Internet sites. If your system has a WAIS client, type

```
swais
```

at the command prompt and hit enter (the "s" stands for "simple"). If it doesn't, telnet to bbs.oit.unc.edu, which is run by the University of North Carolina At the "login:" prompt, type

```
bbs
```

and hit enter. You'll be asked to register and will then get a list of "bulletins," which are various files explaining how the system works.

When done with those, hit your Q key and you'll get another menu. Hit 4 for the "simple WAIS client," and you'll see something like this:

```
SWAIS                  Source Selection Sources: 23#
Server Source Cost
001: [              archie.au] aarnet-resource-guideFree
002: [       archive.orst.edu] aeronauticsFree
003: [nostromo.oes.orst.ed] agricultural-market-newsFree
004: [sun-wais.oit.unc.edu] alt-sys-sunFree
005: [       archive.orst.edu] alt.drugsFree
006: [       wais.oit.unc.edu] alt.gopherFree
007: [sun-wais.oit.unc.edu] alt.sys.sunFree
008: [       wais.oit.unc.edu] alt.waisFree
009: [       archive.orst.edu] archie-orst.eduFree
010: [              archie.au] archie.au-amiga-readmesFree
011: [              archie.au] archie.au-ls-lRtFree
012: [              archie.au] archie.au-mac-readmesFree
013: [              archie.au] archie.au-pc-readmesFree
014: [ pc2.pc.maricopa.edu] ascd-educationFree
015: [              archie.au] au-directory-of-serversFree
016: [    cirm2.univ-mrs.fr] bib-cirmFree
017: [    cmns-sun.think.com] bibleFree
018: [          zenon.inria.fr] bibs-zenon-inria-frFree

Keywords:

<space> selects, w for keywords, arrows move, <return>
searches, q quits, or ?
```

Each line represents a different database (the .au at the end of some of them means they are in Australia; the .fr on the last line represents a database in France). And this is just the first page! If you type a capital K, you'll go to the next page (there are several pages). Hitting a capital J will move you back a page.

The first thing you want to do is tell the WAIS program which databases you want searched. To select a database, move the cursor bar over the line you want (using your down- and up-arrow keys) and hit your space bar. An asterisk will appear next to the line number. Repeat this until you've selected all of the databases you want searched. Then hit your W key, after which you'll be prompted for the keywords you're looking for. You can type in an entire line of these words—separate each with a space, not a comma.

Hit return, and the search begins.

Let's say you're utterly fascinated with wheat. So you might select agricultural-market-news to find its current world price. But you also want to see if it has any religious implications, so you choose the Bible and the Book of Mormon. What do you do with the stuff? Select recipes and usenet-cookbook. Are there any recent Supreme Court decisions involving the plant? Chose supreme-court. How about synonyms? Try roget-thesaurus and just plain thesaurus.

Now hit w and type in wheat. Hit enter, and the WAIS program begins its search. As it looks, it tells you whether any of the databases are offline, and if so, when they might be ready for a search. In about a minute, the program tells you how many hits it's found. Then you get a new menu, that looks something like this:

```
Keywords:
# Score SourceTitleLines
001: [1000] (roget-thesaurus) #465. [results of
comparison. 1] Di 19
002: [1000] (roget-thesaurus) #609. Choice.—N. choice,
option; 36
003: [1000] (roget-thesaurus) #465. [results of compari-
son. 1] Di 19
004: [1000] (roget-thesaurus) #609. Choice.—N. choice,
option; 36
005: [1000] (recipes) aem@mthvax Re: MONTHLY:
Rec.Food.Recipes 425
006: [1000] ( Book_of_Mormon) Mosiah 9:96
007: [1000] ( Book_of_Mormon) 3 Nephi 18:185
008: [1000] (agricultural-ma) Re: JO GR115, WEEKLY
GRAIN82
009: [ 822] (agricultural-ma) Re: WA CB351 PROSPECTIVE
PLANTINGS 552
010: [ 800] ( recipes) kms@apss.a Re: REQUEST: Wheat-
free, Suga 35
011: [ 750] (agricultural-ma) Re: WA CB101 CROP PRODUC-
TION258
012: [ 643] (agricultural-ma) Re: SJ GR850 DAILY NAT GRN
SUM72
013: [ 400] ( recipes) pat@jaamer Re: VEGAN: Honey Gra-
nola63
```

```
014: [ 400] ( recipes) jrtrint@pa Re: OVO-LACTO: Sour-
dough/Trit 142
```

Each of these represents an article or citation that contains the word *wheat,* or some related word. Move the cursor bar (with the down- and up-arrow keys) to the one you want to see, hit enter, and it will begin to appear on your screen. The "score" is a WAIS attempt to gauge how closely the citing matches your request. Doesn't look like the Supreme Court has had anything to say about the plant of late!

Now think of how much time you would have spent logging onto various databases just to find these relatively trivial examples.

8.6 The World-Wide Web

Developed by researchers at the European Particle Physics Laboratory in Geneva, the World-Wide Web is somewhat similar to a WAIS. But it's designed on a system known as hypertext. Words in one document are "linked" to other documents. It's sort of like sitting with an ency- clopedia—you read an article, see a reference that intrigues you, and so flip the pages to look up that reference.

To try the World-Wide Web, telnet to this site:

```
info.cern.ch
```

No log-in is needed. When you connect, you'll see something like this:

```
                         Welcome to CERN
The World-Wide Web: CERN entry point

CERN is the European Particle Physics Laboratory in Ge-
neva, Switzerland. Select by number information here, or
elsewhere.

Help[1]               About this program

World-Wide Web[2]     About the W3 global information
                      initiative.

CERN information[3]   Information from and about this site

Particle Physics[4]   Other HEP sites with information
                      servers
```

```
Other Subjects[5]        Catalogue of all online information
                         by subject.
                         Also: by server type[6] .
```

```
** CHECK OUT X11 BROWSER "ViolaWWW": ANON FTP TO
info.cern.ch in /pub/www/src *** Still beta, so keep bug
reports calm :-)
```

```
If you use this service frequently, please install this
or any W3 browser on your own machine (see instruc-
tions[7] ). You can configure it to start 1-7, <RETURN>
for more, Quit, or Help:
```

You navigate the web by typing the number next to a given refer-ence. So if you want to know more about the web, hit 2. This is another system that bears playing with.

8.7 Clients, or How to Snare More on the Web

If you are used to plain-vanilla Unix or MS-DOS, then the way these gophers and WAISs work seems quite straightforward. But if you're used to a computer with a graphical interface, such as a Macintosh, an IBM-compatible with Windows, or a Next, you'll probably regard their interfaces as somewhat primitive. And even to a veteran MS-DOS user, the World-Wide Web interface is rather clunky (and some of the documents and files on the Web now use special formatting that would confuse your poor computer).

There are, however, ways to integrate these services into your graphical user interface. In fact, there are now ways to tie into the Internet directly, rather than relying on whatever interface your pub-lic-access system uses, through what are known as "client" programs. These programs provide graphical interfaces for everything from ftp to the World-Wide Web.

There is now a growing number of these "client" programs for everything from ftp to gopher. PSI of Reston, Virginia, which offers nationwide Internet access, in fact, requires its customers to use these programs. Using protocols known as SLIP and PPP, these programs communicate with the Net using the same basic data packets as much larger computers online.

Beyond integration with your own computer's "desktop," client programs let you do more than one thing at once on the net—while you're downloading a large file in one window, you can be chatting with a friend through an Internet chat program in another.

Unfortunately, using a client program can cost a lot of money. Some require you to be connected directly to the Internet through an Ethernet network, for example. Others work through modem protocols, such as SLIP, but public-access sites that allow such access may charge anywhere from $25 to $200 a month extra for the service.

Your system administrator can give you more information on setting up one of these connections.

8.8 When Things Go Wrong

As the Internet grows ever more popular, its resources come under more of a strain. If you try to use gopher in the middle of the day, at least on the East Coast of the United States, you'll sometimes notice that it takes a very long time for particular menus or database searches to come up. Sometimes, you'll even get a message that there are too many people connected to whichever service you're trying to use and so you can't get in. The only alternative is to either try again in 20 minutes or so, or wait until later in the day, when the load might be lower. When this happens in veronica, try one of the other veronica entries.

When you retrieve a file through gopher, you'll sometimes be asked if you want to store it under some ludicrously long name (there go our friends the system administrators again, using 128 characters just because Unix lets them). With certain MS-DOS communications programs, if that name is longer than one line, you won't be able to backspace all the way back to the first line if you want to give it a simpler name. Backspace as far as you can. Then, when you get ready to download it to your home computer, remember that the file name will be truncated on your end, because of MS-DOS's file-naming limitations. Worse, your computer might even reject the whole thing. What to do? Instead of saving it to your home directory, mail it to yourself. It should show up in your mail by the time you exit gopher. Then, use your mail program's command for saving it to your home directory— at which point you can name it anything you want. Now you can download it.

8.9 FYI

David Riggins maintains a list of gophers by type and category. You can find the most recent one at the ftp site ftp.einet.net, in the pub directory. Look for a file with a name like "gopher-jewels.txt." Alternately, you can get on a mailing list to get the latest version sent to your e-mailbox automatically. To subscribe, send a mail message to gopherjewelslist-request@tpis.cactus.org (yep, that first part is all one word). Leave the "subject:" line blank, and as a message, write SUBSCRIBE.

Blake Gumprecht maintains a list of gopher and telnet sites related to, or run by, the government. He posts it every three weeks to the news.answers and soc.answers newsgroups on Usenet. It can also be obtained via anonymous ftp from rtfm.mit.edu, as /pub/usenet/news.answers/us-govt-net-pointers.

Students at the University of Michigan's School of Information and Library Studies recently compiled separate lists of Internet resources in 11 specific areas, from aeronautics to theater. They can be obtained via gopher at gopher.lib.umich.edu, in the "What's New and Featured Resources" menu.

The Usenet newsgroups comp.infosystems.gopher and comp.infosystems.wais are places to go for technical discussions about gophers and WAISs respectively.

The Interpedia project is an attempt to take gopher one step further, by creating an online repository of all of the interesting and useful information availble on the Net and from its users. To get on the mailing list for the project, send an e-mail message, with a "subject:" of "subscribe," to interpedia-request@telerama.lm.com. You can get supporting documentation for the project via anonymous ftp at ftp.lm.com in the pub/interpedia directory.

9 Advanced E-Mail

9.1 The File's in the Mail

E-mail by itself is a powerful tool, and by now you may be sending e-mail messages all over the place. You might even be on a mailing list or two. But there is a lot more to e-mail than just sending messages. If your host system does not have access to ftp, or it doesn't have access to every ftp site on the Net, you can have programs and files sent right to your mailbox. And using some simple techniques, you can use e-mail to send data files such as spreadsheets, or even whole programs, to friends and colleagues around the world.

A key to both is a set of programs known as encoders and decoders. For all its basic power, Net e-mail has a big problem: it can't handle graphics characters or the control codes found in even the simplest of computer programs. Encoders, however, can translate these into forms usable in e-mail, while decoders turn them back into a form that you can actually use. If you are using a Unix-based host system, chances are it already has an encoder and decoder online that you can use. These programs will also let you use programs posted in several Usenet newsgroups, such as comp.binaries.ibm.pc.

If both you and the person with whom you want to exchange files use Unix host systems, you're in luck, because virtually all Unix host systems have encoder/decoder programs online. For now, let's assume that's the case. First, upload the file you want to send to your friend to your host site (ask your system administrator how to upload a file to your name or "home" directory if you don't already know how). Then type

```
uuencode file file > file.uu
```

and hit enter. "File" is the name of the file you want to prepare for mailing, and yes, you have to type the name twice! The > is a Unix command that tells the system to call the "encoded" file "file.uu" (you could actually call it anything you want).

Now to get it into a mail message. The quick and dirty way is to type

```
mail friend
```

where "friend" is your friend's address. At the subject line, type the name of the enclosed file. When you get the blank line, type

```
~r file.uu
```

or whatever you called the file, and hit enter (on some systems, the ~ may not work; if so, ask your system administrator what to use). This inserts the file into your mail message. Hit control-D, and your file is on its way!

On the other end, when your friend goes into her mailbox, she should transfer it to her home directory. Then she should type

```
uudecode file.name
```

and hit enter. This creates a new file in her name directory with whatever name you originally gave it. She can then download it to her own computer. Before she can actually use it, though, she'll have to open it up with a text processor and delete the mail header that has been "stamped" on it. If you use a mailer program that automatically appends a "signature," tell her about that so she can delete that as well.

9.2 Receiving Files

If somebody sends you a file through the mail, you'll have to go through a couple of steps to get it into a form you can actually use. If you are using the simple mail program, go into mail and type

```
w # file.name
```

where # is the number of the message you want to transfer and file.name is what you want to call the resulting file. In pine, call up the message and hit your O key and then E. You'll then be asked for a file name. In elm, call up the message and hit your S key. You'll get something that looks like this:

```
=file.request
```

Type a new file name and hit enter (if you hit enter without typing a file name, the message will be saved to another mail folder, not your home directory).

In all three cases, exit the mail program to return to your host system's command line. Because the file has been encoded for mail delivery, you now have to run a decoder. At the command line, type

```
uudecode file.name
```

where file.name is the file you created while in mail. Uudecode will create a new, uncompressed binary file. In some cases, you may have to run it through some other programs (for example, if it is in "tar" form), but generally it should now be ready for you to download to your own computer (on which you might then have to run a decompressor program such as PKXZIP).

9.3 Sending Files to Non-Internet Sites

What if your friend connects only with a non-Unix system, such as CompuServe or MCIMail? There are programs available for MS-DOS, Apple, and Amiga computers that will encode and decode files. Of course, since you can't send one of these programs to your friend via e-mail (how would she unencode it?), you'll have to mail (the old-fashioned way) or give her a diskette with the program on it first. Then, she can get the file by e-mail and go through the previous process (only on her own computer) to get a usable file. Remember to give her an encoder program as well, if she wants to send you files in return.

For MS-DOS machines, you'll want to get uunecode.com and uudecode.com. Both can be found through anonymous ftp at wuarchive.wustl.edu in the /mirrors/msdos/starter directory. The MS-DOS version is as easy to use as the Unix one: Just type

```
uudecode filename.ext
```

and hit enter.

Mac users should get a program called uutool, which can be found in the info-mac/util directory on sumex-aim.stanford.edu.

Think twice before sending somebody a giant file. Although large sites connected directly to the Internet can probably handle mega-files, many smaller systems cannot. Some commercial systems, such as CompuServe and MCIMail, limit the size of mail messages their users can receive. Fidonet doesn't even allow encoded messages. In general, a file size of 30,000 or so bytes is a safe upper limit for non-Internet systems.

9.4 Getting FTP Files via E-Mail

To help people without ftp access, a number of ftp sites have set up mail servers (also known as archive servers) that allow you to get files via e-mail. You send a request to one of these machines and they send back the file you want. As with ftp, you'll be able to find everything from historical documents to software (but please note that if you do have access to ftp, that method is always quicker and ties up fewer resources than using e-mail).

Some interesting or useful mail servers include the following:

mail-server@rtfm.mit.edu Files of "frequently asked questions" related to Usenet; state-by-state lists of U.S. representatives and senators and their addresses and office phone numbers.

archive-server@eff.org Information about the Electronic Frontier Foundation; documents about legal issues on the Net.

archive-server@cs.widener.edu Back copies of the *Computer Underground Digest* and every possible fact you could want to know about *The Simpsons.*

netlib@uunet.uu.net Programs for many types of personal computers; archives of past postings from many Usenet newsgroups.

archive-server@ames.arc.nasa.gov Space-related text and graphics (GIF-format) files.

service@nic.ddn.mil Detailed information about Internet.

Most mail servers work pretty much the same—you send an e-mail message that tells them what file you want and how you want it sent to you. The most important command is "send," which tells the computer you want it to send you a particular file.

First, though, you'll need to know where the mail server stores that file, because you have to tell it which directory or subdirectory it's in. There are a couple of ways to do this. You can send an e-mail message to the archive-server that consists of one line:

```
index
```

The server will then send you a directory listing of its main, or root, directory. You'll then have to send a second message to the archive server with one line:

```
index directory/subdirectory
```

where directory/subdirectory is the directory path for which you want a listing. An alternative is to send an e-mail message to our old friend archie, which should send you back the file's exact location on the archive server (along with similar listings for all the other sites that may have the file, however).

Once you have the file name and its directory path, compose a message to the archive server like this:

```
send directory/subdirectory/file
```

Send off the message, and, anywhere from a few minutes to a couple of days later, you'll find a new message in your mailbox: a copy of the file you requested. The exact time it will take a file to get to you depends on a variety of factors, including how many requests are in line before yours (mail servers can only process so many requests at a time) and the state of the connections between the server and you.

Seems simple enough. It gets a little more complicated when you request a program rather than a document. Programs or other files that contain unusual characters or lines longer than 130 characters (graphics files, for example) require special processing by the mail server to ensure they are transmitted via e-mail. Then you'll have to run them through at least one converter program to put them in a form you can actually use. To ensure that a program or other "non-mailable" file actually gets to you, include another line in your e-mail message to the server:

```
encoder
```

This converts the file into an encoded form. To decode it, you'll first have to transfer the file message into a file in your home directory.

One further complication comes when you request a particularly long file. Many Net sites can only handle so much mail at a time. To make sure you get the entire file, tell the mail server to break it up into smaller pieces, with another line in your e-mail request like this:

```
size 100000
```

This gives the mail server the maximum size, in bytes, of each file segment. This particular size is good for UUCP sites. Internet and Bitnet sites can generally go up to 300000. When you get all of these files in mail, transfer them to your home directory. Exit mail and call up each file in your host system's text processor and delete each one's entire header and footer (or "signature" at the end). When done with this, at your host system's command line, type

```
cat file1 file2 > bigfile
```

where file1 is the first file, file2 the second file, and so on. The > tells your host system to combine them into a new megafile called bigfile (or whatever you want to call it). After you save the file to your home directory (see section 9.2), you can then run uudecode, tar, etc. One word of caution, though: if the file you want is long enough that it has to be broken into pieces, think of how much time it's going to take you to download the whole thing—especially if you're using a 2400-baud modem!

There are a number of other mail servers. To get a list, send an e-mail message to mail-server@rtfm.mit.edu:

```
send usenet/comp.sources.wanted/How_to_find_sources_
(READ_THIS_BEFORE_POSTING)
```

You'll have to spell it exactly as listed above, only write it as one long line with no spaces. Some mail servers use different software, which will require slightly different commands than the ones listed here. In general, if you send a message to a mail server that says only

```
help
```

you should get back a file detailing all of its commands.

But what if the file you want is not on one of these mail servers? That's where ftpmail comes in. Run by Digital Equipment Corp. in California, this service can connect to almost any ftp site in the world, get the file you want, and then mail it to you. Using it is fairly simple—you send an e-mail message to ftpmail that includes a series of commands telling the system where to find the file you want and how to format it to mail to you.

Compose an e-mail message to this address:

```
ftpmail@decwrl.dec.com
```

Leave the "subject:" line blank. Inside the message, there are several commands you can give. The first line should be

```
reply address
```

where "address" is your e-mail address. The next line should be

```
connect host
```

where "host" is the system that has the file you want (for example: wuarchive.wustl.edu). Other commands you should consider using are "binary" (required for program files), "compress" (reduces the file size for quicker transmission), and "uuencode" (which encodes the file so you can do something with it when it arrives). The last line of your message should be the word "quit."

Let's say you want a copy of the U.S. Constitution. Using archie, you've found a file called, surprise, constitution, at the ftp site archive.cis.ohio-state.edu, in the /pub/firearms/politics/rkba directory. You'd send a message to ftpmail@decwrl.dec.com that looks like this:

```
reply adamg@world.std.com
connect archive.cis.ohio-state.edu
binary
compress
uuencode
get pub/firearms/politics/rkba/constitution
quit
```

When you get the file in your mailbox, use the previous procedure for copying it to a file. Run it through uudecode. Then type

```
uncompress file.name
```

to make it usable.

Since this was a text file, you could have changed the "binary" to "ascii" and then eliminated the "uuencode" file. For programs, though, you'll want to keep these lines. One caveat with ftpmail: it has become such a popular service that it could take a week or more for your requested files to arrive.

9.5 The All-Knowing Oracle

One other thing you can do through e-mail is consult with the Usenet Oracle. You can ask the Oracle anything at all and get back an answer (whether you'll like the answer is another question).

First, you'll want to get instructions on how to address the Oracle (he, or she, or it is very particular about such things and likes being addressed in august, solemn, and particularly sycophantic tones). Start an e-mail message to this address:

```
oracle@iuvax.cs.indiana.edu
```

In the "subject:" line, type

```
help
```

and hit enter. You don't actually have to say anything in the message itself—at least not yet. Hit control-D to send off your request for help. Within a few hours, the Oracle will mail you back detailed instructions. It's a fairly long file, so before you start reading it, turn on your communications software's logging function, to save it to your computer (or save the message to a file on your host system's home directory and then download the file). After you've digested it, you can compose your question to the Oracle. Mail it to the previous address, only this time with a subject line that describes your question. Expect an answer within a couple of days. And don't be surprised if you also find a question in your mailbox—the Oracle extracts payment by making seekers of knowledge answer questions as well!

10 News of the World

10.1 Clarinet: AP, Dave Barry, and Dilbert

Usenet "newsgroups" can be something of a misnomer. They may be interesting, informative, and educational, but they are often not news, at least, not the way most people would think of them. But there are several sources of news and sports on the Net.

One of the largest is Clarinet, a company in Cupertino, California, that distributes wire-service news and columns, along with a news service devoted to computers and even the Dilbert comic strip, in Usenet form.

Distributed in Usenet form, Clarinet stories and columns are organized into more than a hundred newsgroups (in this case, a truly appropriate name), some of them with an extremely narrow focus, for example, clari.news.gov.taxes. The general news and sports come from Associated Press, the computer news from the NewsBytes service, the features from several syndicates.

Because Clarinet charges for its service, not all host systems carry its articles. Those that do carry them as Usenet groups starting with "clari." As with other Usenet hierarchies, these are named starting with broad area and ending with more specific categories. Some of these include business news (clari.biz); general national and foreign news, politics, and the like (clari.news); sports (clari.sports); columns by Mike Royko, Miss Manners, Dave Barry, and others (clari.feature); and NewsBytes computer and telecommunications reports (clari.nb). Because Clarinet started in Canada, there is a separate set of clari.canada newsgroups. The clari.nb newsgroups are divided into specific computer types (clari.nb.apple, for example).

Clari newsgroups feature stories updated around the clock. There are even a couple of "bulletin" newsgroups for breaking stories:

clari.news.bulletin and clari.news.urgent. Clarinet also sets up new newsgroups for breaking stories that become ongoing ones (such as major natural disasters, coups in large countries, and the like).

Occasionally, you will see stories in clari newsgroups that just don't seem to belong there. Stories about former Washington, D.C., mayor Marion Barry, for example, often wind interspersed among columns by Dave Barry. This happens because of the way wire services work. AP uses three-letter codes to route its stories to the newspapers and radio stations that make up most of its clientele, and harried editors on deadline sometimes punch in the wrong code.

10.2 Reuters

This is roughly the British equivalent of Associated Press. Msen, a public-access site in Michigan, currently feeds Reuters dispatches into a series of Usenet-style conferences. If your site subscribes to this service, look for newsgroups with names that begin in msen.reuters.

10.3 USA Today

If your host system doesn't carry the clari or msen.reuters newsgroups, you might be able to keep up with the news a different way over the Net. *USA Today* has been something of an online newspaper pioneer, selling its stories to bulletin board and online systems across the country for several years. Cleveland Free-Net provides the online version of *USA Today* (along with all its other services) for free. Currently, the paper publishes only five days a week, so you'll have to get your weekend news fix elsewhere.

```
Telnet: freenet-in-a.cwru.edu or
        freenet-in-b.cwru.edu or
        freenet-in-c.cwru.edu
```

After you connect and log in, look for this menu entry: NPTN/USA TODAY HEADLINE NEWS. Type the number next to it and hit enter. You'll then get a menu listing a series of broad categories, such as sports and telecommunications. Choose one, and you'll get yet another menu, listing the ten most recent dates of publication. Each of these contains one-paragraph summaries of the day's news in that particular subject.

10.4 National Public Radio

Look in the alt.radio.networks.npr newsgroup in Usenet for summaries of NPR news shows such as "All Things Considered." This newsgroup is also a place to discuss the network and its shows, personalities, and policies.

10.5 The World Today, from Belarus to Brazil

Radio Free Europe and Radio Liberty are American radio stations that broadcast to the former Communist countries of eastern Europe. Every day, their news departments prepare a summary of news in those countries, which is then disseminated via the Net, through a Bitnet mailing list and a Usenet newsgroup.

To have the daily digests sent directly to your e-mailbox, send a message to this address:

```
listserv@ubvm.cc.buffalo.edu
```

Leave the subject line blank, and as a message, write this:

```
subscribe rferl-l Your Name
```

Alternately, look for the bulletins in the Usenet newsgroup misc.news-east-europe.rferl.

The Voice of America, a government broadcasting service aimed at other countries, provides transcripts of its English-language news reports through both gopher and anonymous ftp. For the former, use gopher to connect to this address:

```
gopher.voa.gov
```

and for the latter, to this address:

```
ftp.voa.gov
```

Daily Brazilian news updates are available (in Portuguese) from the University of Sao Paulo. Use anonymous ftp to connect:

```
uspif.if.usp.br
```

Use cd to switch to the whois directory. Get the news.new file.

Daily summaries of news reports from France (in French) are availble on the National Capital FreeNet in Ottawa, Ontario. Telnet to

```
freenet.carleton.ca
```

and log on as guest. At the main menu, select the number for "The Newsstand" and then "La presse de France."

10.6 E-Mailing News Organizations

A number of newspapers, television stations, and networks and other news organizations now encourage readers and viewers to communicate with them electronically, via Internet e-mail addresses. They include the following:

The Middlesex News, Framingham, Mass.	sysop@news.ci.net
The Boston Globe	voxbox@globe.com
WCVB-TV, Boston, Mass.	wcvb@aol.com
NBC News, New York, N.Y.	nightly@nbc.com
The Ottawa Citizen, Ottawa, Ont.	ottawa-citizen@freenet.carleton.ca
CJOH-TV, Ottawa, Ont.	ab363@freenet.carleton.ca
St. Petersburg (Fla.) Times	73174.3344@compuserve.com
Illinois Issues, Springfield, Ill.	gherardi@sangamon.edu
WTVF-TV, Nashville, Tenn.	craig.ownsby@nashville.com
Santa Cruz County (Calif.) Sentinel	sented@cruzio.com
Morning Journal, Lorain, Ohio	mamjornl@freenet.lorain.oberlin.edu
WCCO-TV, Minneapolis, Minn.	wccotv@mr.net
Tico Times, Costa Rica	ttimes@huracon.cr

10.7 FYI

The clari.net.newusers newsgroup on Usenet provides a number of articles about Clarinet and ways of finding news stories of interest to you.

To discuss the future of newspapers and newsrooms in the new electronic medium, subscribe to the Computer Assisted Reporting and Research mailing list on Bitnet. Send a mail message of

```
Subscribe carr-l Your Name
```

to listserv@ulkyvm.bitnet.

11   IRC, MUDs, and Other Things That Are More Fun Than They Sound

Many Net systems provide access to a series of interactive services that let you hold live "chats" or play online games with people around the world. To find out if your host system offers these, you can ask your system administrator or just try them—if nothing happens, then your system does not provide them. In general, if you can use telnet and ftp, chances are good you can use these services as well.

11.1   Talk

This is the Net equivalent of a telephone conversation and requires that both you and the person you want to talk to have access to this function and are online at the same time. To use it, type

```
talk user@site.name
```

where user@site.name is the e-mail address of the other person. She will see something like this on her screen:

```
talk: connection requested by yourname@site.name
talk: respond with: talk yourname@site.name
```

To start the conversation, she should then type (at her host system's command line):

```
talk yourname@site.name
```

where that is your e-mail address. Both of you will then get a top and bottom window on your screen. She will see everything you type in one window; you'll see everything she types in the other. To disconnect, hit control-C.

One note: Public-access sites that use Sun computers sometimes have trouble with the talk program. If talk does not work, try typing

```
otalk
```

or

```
ntalk
```

instead. However, the party at the other end will have to have the same program online for the connection to work.

11.2 Internet Relay Chat

IRC is a program that lets you hold live keyboard conversations with people around the world. It's a lot like an international CB radio—it even uses "channels." Type something on your computer, and it's instantly echoed around the world to whoever happens to be on the same channel with you. You can join in existing public group chats or set up your own. You can even create a private channel for yourself and as few as one or two other people. And just like on a CB radio, you can give yourself a unique "handle" or nickname.

IRC currently links host systems in 20 different countries, from Australia to Hong Kong to Israel. Unfortunately, it's like telnet—either your site has it or it doesn't. If your host system does have it, just type

```
irc
```

and hit enter. You'll get something like this:

```
*** Connecting to port 6667 of server world.std.com
*** Welcome to the Internet Relay Network, adamg
*** Your host is world.std.com, running version 2.7.1e+4
*** You have new mail.
*** If you have not already done so, please read the new
user information with +/HELP NEWUSER
*** This server was created Sat Apr 18 1992 at 16:27:02
EDT
*** There are 364 users on 140 servers
*** 45 users have connection to the twilight zone
*** There are 124 channels.
*** I have 1 clients and 3 servers
MOTD - world.std.com Message of the Day -
MOTD - Be careful out there . . .
MOTD -
```

```
MOTD - ->Spike
* End of /MOTD command.

23:13 [1] adamg [Mail: 32] * type /help for help
```

You are now in channel 0, the "null" channel, in which you can look up various help files, but not much else. As you can see, IRC takes over your entire screen. The top of the screen is where messages will appear. The last line is where you type IRC commands and messages. All IRC commands begin with a /. The slash tells the computer you are about to enter a command, rather than a message. To see what channels are available, type

```
/list
```

and hit enter. You'll get something like this:

```
*** Channel     Users          Topic
*** #Money      1 School CA$H (/msg SOS_AID help)
*** #Gone       1 ---->> Gone with the wind!!! ------>>>>>
*** #mee        1
*** #eclipse    1
*** #hiya2
*** #saigon     4
*** #screwed    3
*** #z2
*** #comix      1 LET'S TALK 'BOUT COMIX!!!!!
*** #Drama      1
*** #RayTrace   1 Rendering to Reality and Back
*** #NeXT       1
*** #wicca      4 Mr. Potato Head, R. I. P.
*** #dde^mhe`   1 o'ng chay? mo*? . . . ba` con o*iiii
*** #jgm        1
*** #ucd        1
*** #Maine      2
*** #Snuffland  1
*** #p/g!       4
*** #DragonSrv  1
```

Because IRC allows for a large number of channels, the list might scroll off your screen, so you might want to turn on your computer's screen capture to capture the entire list. Note that the channels always have names, instead of numbers. Each line in the listing tells you the channel name, the number of people currently in it, and whether there's a specific topic for it. To switch to a particular channel, type

```
/join #channel
```

where "#channel" is the channel name, and hit enter. Some "public" channels actually require an invitation from somebody already on them. To request an invitation, type

```
/who #channel-name
```

where channel-name is the name of the channel, and hit enter. Then ask someone with an @ next to his or her name if you can join in. Note that whenever you enter a channel, you have to include the #. Choose one with a number of users, so you can see IRC in action.

If it's a busy channel, as soon as you join it, the top of your screen will quickly be filled with messages. Each will start with a person's IRC nickname, followed by the message.

It may seem awfully confusing at first. There could be two or three conversations going on at the same time, and sometimes the messages will come in so fast you'll wonder how you can read them all.

Eventually, though, you'll get into the rhythm of the channel and things will begin to make more sense. You might even want to add your two cents (in fact, don't be surprised if a message to you shows up on your screen right away; on some channels, newcomers are welcomed immediately). To enter a public message, simply type it on that bottom line (the computer knows it's a message because you haven't started the line with a slash) and hit enter.

Public messages have a user's nickname in brackets, like this:

```
<tomg>
```

If you receive a private message from somebody, his name will be between asterisks, like this:

```
*tomg*
```

11.3 IRC Commands

Note: Hit enter after each command.

/away	When you're called away to put out a grease fire in the kitchen, issue this command to let others know you're still connected but just away from your terminal or computer for a while.
/help	Brings up a list of commands for which there is a help file. You will get a "topic:" prompt. Type in the subject for which you want information and hit enter. Hit enter by itself to exit help.
/invite	Asks another IRC to join you in a conversation.

/invite fleepo #hottub

would send a message to fleepo asking him to join you on the #hottub channel. The channel name is optional.

/join	Use this to switch to or create a particular channel, like this:

`/join #hottub`

If one of these channels exists and is not a private one, you will enter it. Otherwise, you have just created it. Note you have to use a # as the first character.

/list	This will give you a list of all available public channels, their topics (if any), and the number of users currently on them. Hidden and private channels are not shown.
/m name	Sends a private message to that user.
/mode	This lets you determine who can join a channel you've created.

`/mode #channel +s`

creates a secret channel.

`/mode #channel +p`

makes the channel private.

/nick	This lets you change the name by which others see you.

```
/nick fleepo
```

would change your name for the present session to fleepo. People can still use /whois to find your e-mail address. If you try to enter a channel where somebody else is already using that nickname, IRC will ask you to select another name.

/query

This sets up a private conversation between you and another IRC user. To do this, type

```
/query nickname
```

Every message you type after that will go only to that person. If she then types

```
/query nickname
```

where nickname is yours, then you have established a private conversation. To exit this mode, type

```
/query
```

by itself. While in query mode, you and the other person can continue to "listen" to the discussion on whatever public channels you were on, although neither of you will be able to respond to any of the messages there.

/quit   Exits IRC.

/signoff   Exits IRC.

/summon   Asks somebody connected to a host system with IRC to join you on IRC. You must use the person's entire e-mail address.

```
/summon fleepo@foo.bar.com
```

would send a message to fleepo asking him to start IRC. Usually not a good idea to just summon people unless you know they're already amenable to the idea; otherwise you may wind up annoying them no end. This command does not work on all sites.

/topic

When you've started a new channel, use this command to let others know what it's about.

`/topic #Amiga`

would tell people who use /list that your channel is meant for discussing Amiga computers.

/who <chan>

Shows you the e-mail address of people on a particular channel.

`/who #foo`

would show you the addresses of everybody on channel foo.

`/who`

by itself shows you every e-mail address for every person on IRC at the time, although be careful: on a busy night you might get a list of five hundred names!

/whois

Use this to get some information about a specific IRC user or to see who is online.

`/whois nickname`

will give you the e-mail address for the person using that nickname.

`/whois *`

will list everybody on every channel.

/whowas

Similar to /whois; gives information for people who recently signed off IRC.

11.4 IRC in Times of Crisis

IRC has become a new medium for staying on top of really big breaking news. In 1993, when Russian lawmakers barricaded them-selves inside the parliament building, some enterprising Muscovites and a couple of Americans set up a "news channel" on IRC to relay first-person accounts direct from Moscow. The channel was set up to provide a continuous loop of information, much like all-news radio stations that cycle through the day's news every 20 minutes. In 1994, Los Angeles residents set up a similar channel to relay information related to the Northridge earthquake. In both cases, logs of the channels were archived somewhere on the Net, for those unable to "tune in" live.

How would you find such channels in the future? Use the /list command to scroll through the available channels. If one has been set up to discuss a particular breaking event, chances are you'll see a brief description next to the channel name that will tell you that's the place to tune.

11.5 MUDs

Multiple-User Dimensions or Dungeons (MUDs) take IRC into the realm of fantasy. MUDs are live, role-playing games in which you assume a new identity and enter an alternate reality through your keyboard. As you explore this other world, through a series of simple commands (such as "look," "go," and "take"), you'll run across other users, who may engage you in a friendly discussion, enlist your aid in some quest, or try to kill you for no apparent reason.

Each MUD has its own personality and creator (or God) who was willing to put in the long hours required to establish the particular MUD's rules, laws of nature, and information databases. Some MUDs stress the social aspects of online communications—users frequently gather online to chat and join together to build new structures or even entire realms. Others are closer to "Dungeons and Dragons" and are filled with sorcerers, dragons, and evil people out to keep you from completing your quest—through murder if necessary.

Many MUDs (there are also related games known as MUCKs, MUSEs, and MOOs) require you to apply in advance, through e-mail, for a character name and password. One that lets you look around first, though, is HoloMuck at McGill University in Montreal. The premise of this game is that you arrive in the middle of Tanstaafl, a city on the planet Holo. You have to find a place to live (otherwise you get thrown into the homeless shelter), and then you can begin exploring. Magic is allowed on this world, but only outside the city limits. Get bored with the city, and you can roam the rest of the world or even take a trip into orbit (of course, all this takes money; you can either wait for your weekly salary or take a trip to the city casino).

Once you become familiar with the city and get your own character, you can even begin erecting your own building (or subway line, or almost anything else).

To connect, telnet to this address:

```
collatz.mcrcim.mcgill.edu 5757
```

When you connect, type

```
connect guest guest
```

and hit enter. This connects you to the "guest" account, which has a password of "guest." You'll see this:

```
The Homeless Shelter(#22Rna)
You wake up in the town's Homeless Shelter, where va-
grants are put for protective holding. Please don't
sleep in public places--there are plenty of open apart-
ments available. Type 'apartments' to see how to get to
an apartment building with open vacancies.
There is a small sign on the wall here, with helpful in-
formation. Type 'look sign' to read it.
The door is standing open for your return to respectable
society. Simply walk 'out' to the center.
```

Of course, you want to join respectable society, but first you want to see what that sign says. So you type

```
look sign
```

and hit enter, which brings up a list of some basic commands. Then you type

```
out
```

followed by enter, which brings up this:

```
You slip out the door, and head southeast . . .

Tanstaafl Center
This is the center of the beautiful town of Tanstaafl.
High Street runs north and south into residential areas,
while Main Street runs east and west into business dis-
tricts.
SW: is Tanstaafl Towers. Please claim an apartment . . .
no sleeping in public!
```

```
SE: the Public Library offers both information and enter-
tainment.
NW: is the Homeless Shelter, formerly the Town Jail.
NE: is Town Hall, site of several important services, in-
cluding: Public Message Board, Bureau of Land Management
(with maps and regulations), and other governmental/ bu-
reaucratic help.
Down: Below a sign marked with both red and blue large
letter 'U's, a staircase leads into an underground sub-
way passage.
(Feel free to 'look' in any direction for more
information.)
[Obvious exits: launch, d, nw, se, w, e, n, s, ne, sw]
Contents:
Instructions for newcomers
Directional signpost
Founders' statue
```

To see "Instructions for newcomers," type

```
look Instructions for newcomers
```

and hit enter. You could do the same for "Directional signpost" and "Founders' statue." Then type

```
SW
```

and enter to get to Tanstaafl Towers, the city housing complex, where you have to claim an apartment (you may have to look around; many will already be occupied). And now it's off to explore Holo! One command you'll want to keep in mind is "take." Periodically, you'll come across items that, when you take them, will confer certain abilities or powers on you. If you type

```
help
```

and enter, you'll get a list of files you can read to learn more about the MUD's commands.

The "say" command lets you talk to other players publicly. For example,

```
say Hey, I'm here!
```

would be broadcast to everybody else in the room with you. If you want to talk to just one particular person, use "whisper" instead of "say."

```
whisper agora=Hey, I'm here!
```

would be heard only by agora. Another way to communicate with people regardless of where on the world they are is through your pager. If you suddenly see yours go off while visiting, chances are it's a wizard checking to see if you need any help. To read his message, type

```
page
```

To send him a message, type

```
page name=message
```

where name is the wizard's name (it'll be in the original message).

Other MUDs and MUCKs may have different commands, they but generally use the same basic idea of letting you navigate through relatively simple English commands.

When you connect to a MUD, choose your password as carefully as you would one for your host system; alas, there are MUD crackers who enjoy trying to break into other people's MUD accounts. And never, never use the same password as the one you use on your host system!

MUDs can prove highly addicting. "The jury is still out on whether MUDding is 'just a game' or 'an extension of real life with gamelike qualities,'" says Jennifer Smith, an active MUD player who wrote an FAQ on the subject.

She adds one caution: "You shouldn't do anything that you wouldn't do in real life, even if the world is a fantasy world. The important thing to remember is that it's the fantasy world of possibly hundreds of people, and not just yours in particular. There's a human being on the other side of each and every wire! Always remember that you may meet these other people some day, and they may break your nose. People who treat others badly gradually build up bad reputations and eventually receive the NO FUN Stamp of Disapproval."

11.6 Go, Go, Go (and Chess, Too)!

Fancy a good game of go or chess? You no longer have to head for the nearest park with a board in hand. The Internet has a couple of machines that let you engage people from around the world in your favorite board games. Or, if you prefer, you can watch matches in progress.

To play go:

```
telnet hellspark.wharton.upenn.edu 6969
log on as: guest
```

You'll find prompts to various online help files to get you started.

For a chess match:

```
telnet news.panix.com 5000
log on as: guest
```

You'll find prompts for online help files on the system, which lets you choose your skill level.

11.7 The Other Side of the Coin

All is not fun and games on the Net. Like any community, the Net has its share of obnoxious characters who seem to exist only to make your life miserable (you've already met some of them in chapter 4). There are people who seem to spend a bit more time on the Net than many would find healthy. It also has its criminals. Clifford Stoll writes in *The Cuckoo's Egg* how he tracked a team of German hackers who were breaking into U.S. computers and selling the information they found to the Soviets. Robert Morris, a Cornell University student, was convicted of unleashing a "worm" program that effectively disabled several thousand computers connected to the Internet.

Of more immediate concern to the average Net user are crackers who seek to find other's passwords to break into Net systems and people who infect programs on ftp sites with viruses.

There is a widely available program known as "Crack" that can decipher user passwords composed of words that might be found in a dictionary (this is why you shouldn't use such passwords). Short of that, there are the annoying types who take a special thrill in trying to make you miserable. The best advice in dealing with them is to count to ten and then ignore them—like juveniles everywhere, most of their fun comes in seeing how upset you can get.

Meanwhile, two Cornell University students pleaded guilty in 1992 to uploading virus-infected Macintosh programs to ftp sites. If you plan to try out large amounts of software from ftp sites, it might be wise to download or buy a good antiviral program.

But can law enforcement go too far in seeking out the criminals? The Electronic Frontier Foundation was founded in large part in response to a series of government raids against an alleged gang of hackers. The raids resulted in the near bankruptcy of one game company never alleged to have had anything to do with the hackers, when the government seized its computers and refused to give them back. The case against another alleged participant collapsed in court when his attorney showed that the "proprietary" and supposedly hacked information he printed in an electronic newsletter was actually available via an 800 number for about $13—from the phone company from which that data was taken.

11.8 FYI

You can find discussions about IRC in the alt.irc newsgroup.

"A Discussion on Computer Network Conferencing," by Darren Reed (May, 1992), provides a theoretical background on why conferencing systems such as IRC are a Good Thing. It's available through ftp at nic.ddn.mil in the rfc directory as rfc1324.txt.

Every Friday, Scott Goehring posts a new list of MUDs and related games and their telnet addresses in the newsgroup rec.games.mud.announce. There are several other mud newsgroups related to specific types of MUDs, including rec.games.mud.social, rec.games.mud.adventure, rec.games.mud.tiny, rec.games.mud.diku, and rec.games.mud.lp.

For a good overview of the impact on the Internet of the Morris Worm, read "Virus Highlights Need for Improved Internet Management," by the U.S. General Accounting Office (June, 1989). You can get a copy via ftp from cert.sei.cmu.edu in the pub/virus-l/docs directory. It's listed as gao_rpt.

Clifford Stoll describes how the Internet works, and how he tracked a group of KGB-paid German hackers through it, in *The Cuckoo's Egg: Tracking a Spy through the Maze of Computer Espionage*, Doubleday (1989).

12   Education and the Net

12.1   The Net in the Classroom

If you're a teacher, you've probably already begun to see the potential the Net has for use in the class. Usenet, ftp, and telnet have tremendous educational potential, from keeping up with world events to arranging international science experiments.

Because the Net now reaches so many countries and often stays online even when the phones go down, you and your students can "tune in" to first-hand accounts during international conflicts. Look at your system's list of Usenet soc.culture groups to see if there is one about the country or region you're interested in. Even in peacetime, these newsgroups can be great places to find people from countries you might be studying.

The biggest problem may be getting accounts for your students, if you're not lucky enough to live within the local calling area of a Free-Net system. Many colleges and universities, however, are willing to discuss providing accounts for secondary students at little or no cost. Several states, including California and Texas, have Internet-linked networks for teachers and students.

12.2   Some Specific Resources for Students and Teachers

In addition, there are a number of resources on the Internet aimed specifically at elementary and secondary students and teachers. You can use these to set up science experiments with classes in another country, learn how to use computers in the classroom, or keep up with the latest advances in teaching everything from physics to physical education.

Among them are the following:

AskERIC

Run by the Educational Resource and Information Center, AskERIC provides a way for educators, librarians, and others interested in K-12 education to get more information about virtually everything. The center maintains an e-mail address (askeric@ericir.syr.edu) for questions and promises answers within 48 hours. It also maintains a gopher site that contains digests of questions and answers, lesson plans in a variety of fields, and other educationally related information. The gopher address is ericir.syr.edu.

Health-Ed

A mailing list for health educators. Send a request to health-ed-request@stjhmc.fidonet.org.

K12Net

Begun on the Fidonet hobbyist network, K12Net is now also carried on many Usenet systems and provides a host of interesting and valuable services. These include international chat for students, foreign-language discussions (for example, there are French- and German-only conferences where American students can practice those languages with students from Quebec and Germany). There are also conferences aimed at teachers of specific subjects, from physical education to physics. The K12 network still has limited distribution, so ask your system administrator if your system carries it.

Kidsphere

Kidsphere is a mailing list for elementary and secondary teachers, who use it to arrange joint projects and discuss educational telecommunications. You will find news of new software, lists of sites from which you can get computer-graphics pictures from various NASA satellites and probes, and other news of interest to modem-using teachers.

To subscribe, send a request by e-mail to kidsphere-request@vms.cis.pitt.edu or joinkids-@vms.cis.pitt.edu, and you will start receiving messages within a couple of days.

To contribute to the discussion, send messages to kidsphere@vms.cis.pitt.edu.

KIDS is a spin-off of KIDSPHERE just for students who want to contact students. To subscribe, send a request to joinkids@vms.cis.pitt.edu. To contribute, send messages to kids@vms.-cist.pitt.edu.

Knoxville News-Sentinel Online

Using the newspaper in the electronic classroom. This gopher site lets students and teachers connect to the newspaper, and provides resources for them derived from the newsroom. Use gopher to connect to gopher.opup.org

MicroMUSE

This is an online, futuristic city, built entirely by participants (see chapter 11 for information on MUSEs and MUDs in general). Hundreds of students from all over have participated in this educational exercise, coordinated by MIT. Telnet to michael.ai.mit.edu. Log on as guest and then follow the prompts for more information.

NASA Spacelink

This system, run by NASA in Huntsville, Alabama, provides all sorts of reports and data about NASA, its history, and its various missions, past and present. Telnet spacelink.msfc.nasa.gov or 128.158.13.250.

When you connect, you'll be given an overview of the system and asked to register. The system maintains a large file library of GIF-format space graphics, but note that you can't download these through telnet. If you want to, you have to dial the system directly, at (205) 895- 0028. Many can be obtained through ftp from ames.arc.nasa.gov, however.

Newton

Run by the Argonne National Laboratory, it offers conferences for teachers and students, including one called "Ask a Scientist."

```
Telnet: newton.dep.anl.gov
Log in as: cocotext
```

You'll be asked to provide your name and address. When you get the main menu, hit 4 for the various conferences. The "Ask a Scientist" category lets you ask questions of scientists in fields from biology to earth science. Other categories let you discuss teaching, sports, and computer networks.

OERI

The U.S. Department of Education's Office of Educational Resources and Improvement runs a gopher system that provides numerous educational resources, information, and statistics for teachers. Use gopher to connect to this address:

```
gopher.ed.gov
```

Spacemet
Forum

If your system doesn't carry the K12 conferences but does provide you with telnet, you can reach the conferences through SpaceMet Forum, a bulletin board system aimed at teachers and students that is run by the physics and astronomy department at the University of Massachusetts at Amherst.

```
Telnet: spacemet.phast.umass.edu.
```

When you connect, hit escape once, after which you'll be asked to log on. Like K12Net, SpaceMet Forum began as a Fidonet system, but has since grown much larger. Mort and Helen Sternheim, professors at the university, started SpaceMet as a one-line bulletin board system several years ago to help bolster middle-school science education in nearby towns. In addition to the K12 conferences, SpaceMet carries numerous educationally oriented conferences. It also has a large file library of interest to educators and students, but be aware that getting files to your site could be difficult and maybe even impossible. Unlike most other Internet sites, Spacemet does not use an ftp interface. The Sternheims say ZMODEM sometimes works over the network.

12.3   Usenet and Bitnet in the Classroom

There are numerous Usenet newsgroups of potential interest to teachers and students. As you might expect, many are of a scientific bent. You can find these by typing l sci. in rn or using nngrep sci. for nn. There are now close to 40, with subjects ranging from archaeology to economics (the "dismal science," remember?) to astronomy to nanotechnology (the construction of microscopically small machines).

One thing students will quickly learn from many of these groups: science is not just dull, boring facts. Science is argument and standing your ground and making your case. The Usenet sci. groups encourage critical thinking.

Beyond science, social studies and history classes can keep busy learning about other countries, through the soc.culture newsgroups. Most of these newsgroups originated as ways for expatriates of a given country to keep in touch with their homeland and its culture. In times of crisis, however, these groups often become places to disseminate information from or into the country and to discuss what is happening. From Afghanistan to Yugoslavia, close to 50 countries are now represented on Usenet. To see which groups are available, use l soc.culture. in rn or nngrep soc.culture. for nn.

Several "talk" newsgroups provide additional topical discussions, but teachers should screen them first before recommending them to students. They range from talk.abortion and talk.politics.guns to talk.politics.space and talk.environment.

One caveat: Teachers might want to peruse particular newsgroups before setting their students loose in them. Some have higher levels of flaming and blather than others.

There are also a number of Bitnet discussion groups of potential interest to students and teachers. See chapter 5 for information on finding and subscribing to Bitnet discussion groups. Some with an educational orientation include the following:

biopi-l	ksuvm.bitnet	Secondary biology education
chemed-l	uwf.bitnet	Chemistry education
dts-l	iubvm.bitnet	The Dead Teacher's Society list
phys-l	uwf.bitnet	Discussions for physics teachers

| physhare | psuvm.bitnet | Where physics teachers share resources |
| scimath-l | psuvm.bitnet | Science and math education |

To get a list of ftp sites that carry astronomical images in the GIF graphics format, use ftp to connect to nic.funet.fi. Switch to the /pub/astro/general directory and get the file astroftp.txt. Among the sites listed is ames.arc.nasa.gov, which carries images taken by the Voyager and Galileo probes, among other pictures.

13   Business on the Net

13.1 Setting Up Shop

Back in olden days, oh, before 1990 or so, there were no markets in the virtual community—if you wanted to buy a book, you still had to jump in your car and drive to the nearest bookstore.

This was because, in those days, the Net consisted mainly of a series of government-funded networks on which explicit commercial activity was forbidden. Today, much of the Net is run by private companies, which generally have no such restrictions, and a number of companies have begun experimenting with online "shops" or other services. Many of these shops are run by booksellers, while the services range from delivery of indexed copies of federal documents to an online newsstand that hopes to entice you to subscribe to any of several publications (of the printed-on-paper variety). A number of companies also use Usenet newsgroups (in the biz hierarchy) to distribute press releases and product information.

Still, commercial activity on the Net remains far below that found on other networks, such as CompuServe, with its Electronic Mall, or Prodigy, with its advertisements on almost every screen. In part that's because of the newness and complexity of the Internet as a commercial medium. In part, however, that is because of security concerns. Companies worry about such issues as crackers getting into their system over the network, and many people do not like the idea of sending a credit-card number via the Internet (an e-mail message could be routed through several sites to get to its destination). These concerns could disappear as Net users turn to such means as message encryption and "digital signatures." In the meantime, however, businesses on the Net can still consider themselves something of Internet pioneers.

A couple of public-access sites and a regional network have set up "marketplaces" for online businesses.

The World in Brookline, Massachusetts, currently rents "space" to several bookstores and computer-programming firms, as well as an "adult toy shop." To browse their offerings, use gopher to connect to this address:

```
world.std.com
```

At the main menu, select "Shops on the World."

Msen in Ann Arbor, Michigan, provides its "Msen Marketplace," where you'll find a travel agency and an "Online Career Center" offering help-wanted ads from across the country. Msen also provides an "Internet Business Pages," an online directory of companies seeking to reach the Internet community. You can reach Msen through gopher at this address:

```
gopher.msen.com
```

At the main menu, select "Msen Marketplace."

The Nova Scotia Technology Network runs a "Cybermarket" on its gopher service at this address:

```
nstn.ns.ca
```

There, you'll find an online bookstore that lets you order books through e-mail (to which you'll have to trust your credit-card number) and a similar "virtual record store." Both let you search their wares by keyword or by browsing through catalogs.

Other online businesses include the following:

AnyWare Associates	This Boston company runs an Internet-to-fax gateway that lets you send fax message anywhere in the world via the Internet (for a fee, of course). For more information, write to this address: `sales@awa.com`
Bookstacks Unlimited	This Cleveland bookstore offers a keyword-searchable database of thousands of books for sale. Use telnet to connect to this address: `books.com`

Counterpoint Publishing	Based in Cambridge, Massachusetts, this company's main Internet product is indexed versions of federal journals, including the Federal Register (a daily compendium of government contracts, proposed regulations, and the like). Internet users can browse through recent copies, but complete access will run several thousand dollars a year. Use gopher to connect to

`enews.com`

and select "Counterpoint Publishing."

Dialog	The national database company can be reached through telnet at this address:

`dialog.com`

To log on, however, you will have first had to set up a Dialog account.

Dow Jones News Retrieval	A wire service run by the information company that owns the *Wall Street Journal*. Available via telnet:

`djnr.dowjones.com`

As with Dialog, you need an account to log on.

Infinity Link	Browse book, music, software, video-cassette, and laser-disk catalogs through this system based in Malvern, Pennsylvania. Use gopher to connect:

`columbia.ilc.com`

Log on as: cas

The Internet Company	Sort of a service bureau, this company, based in Cambridge, Massachusetts, is working with several publishers on Internet-related products. Its Electronic Newsstand offers snippets and special subscription rates to a number of national magazines, from the *New Republic* to the *New Yorker*. Use gopher to connect:

`enews.com`

MarketBase   You can try the classified-ads system developed
                            by this company in Santa Barbara, California, by
                            gopher:

                            `mb.com`

O'Reilly and   Best known for its "Nutshell" books on Unix,
Associates   O'Reilly runs three Internet services. The gopher
                            server, at

                            `ora.com`

                            provides information about the company and its
                            books. It posts similar information in the
                            biz.oreilly.announce Usenet newsgroup. Its Global
                            Network Navigator, accessible through the World-
                            Wide Web, is a sort of online magazine that lets
                            users browse through interesting services and
                            catalogs.

13.2 FYI

The com-priv mailing list is the place to discuss issues surrounding
the commercialization and the privatization of the Internet. To subscribe (or unsubscribe), send an e-mail request to com-priv-re-
quest@psi.com.

Mary Cronin's book, *Doing Business on the Internet* (1994, Van Nos-
trand Reinhold), takes a more in-depth look at the subject.

14   Conclusion: The End?

The revolution is just beginning. New communications systems and digital technologies have already meant dramatic changes in the way we live. Think of what is already routine that would have been considered impossible just ten years ago. You can browse through the holdings of your local library—or of libraries halfway around the world—do your banking, and see if your neighbor has gone bankrupt, all through a computer and modem.

Imploding costs coupled with exploding power are bringing ever more powerful computer and digital systems to ever-growing numbers of people. The Net, with its rapidly expanding collection of databases and other information sources, is no longer limited to the industrialized nations of the West; today the web extends from Siberia to Zimbabwe. The cost of computers and modems used to plug into the Net, meanwhile, continues to plummet, making them ever more affordable.

Cyberspace has become a vital part of millions of people's daily lives. People form relationships online, they fall in love, they get married, all because of initial contacts in cyberspace, that ephemeral "place" that transcends national and state boundaries. Business deals are transacted entirely in ASCII. Political and social movements begin online, coordinated by people who could be thousands of miles apart.

Yet this is only the beginning.

We live in an age of communication, yet the various media we use to talk to one another remain largely separate systems. One day, however, your telephone, TV, fax machine, and personal computer will be replaced by a single "information processor" linked to the worldwide Net by strands of optical fiber.

Beyond databases and file libraries, power will be at your fingertips. Linked to thousands, even millions, of like-minded people, you'll be able to participate in social and political movements across the country and around the world.

How does this happen? In part, it will come about through new technologies. High-definition television will require the development of inexpensive computers that can process as much information as today's workstations. Telephone and cable companies will cooperate, or in some cases compete, to bring those fiber-optic cables into your home.

The Clinton administration, arguably the first led by people who know how to use not only computer networks but computers, is pushing for creation of a series of "information superhighways" comparable in scope to the Interstate highway system of the 1950s (one of whose champions in the Senate has a son elected vice-president in 1992).

Right now, we are in the network equivalent of the early 1950s, just before the creation of that massive highway network. Sure, there are plenty of interesting things out there, but you have to meander along two-lane roads, and have a good map, to get to them.

Creation of this new Net will require more than just high-speed channels and routing equipment; it will require a new communications paradigm: the Net as information utility. The Net remains a somewhat complicated and mysterious place. To get something out of the Net today, you have to spend a fair amount of time with a Net veteran or a manual like this. You have to learn such arcana as the vagaries of the Unix cd command.

Contrast this with the telephone, which now also provides access to large amounts of information through push buttons, or a computer network such as Prodigy, which one navigates through simple commands and mouse clicks.

Internet system administrators have begun to realize that not all people want to learn the intricacies of Unix, and that that fact does not make them bad people. We are already seeing the development of simple interfaces that will put the Net's power to use by millions of people. You can already see their influence in the menus of gophers and the World-Wide Web, which require no complex computing skills but which open the gates to thousands of information resources. Mail programs and text editors such as pico and pine promise much of the power of older programs such as emacs at a fraction of the complexity.

Some software engineers are taking this even further, by creating graphical interfaces that will let somebody navigate the Internet just by clicking on the screen with a mouse or by calling up an easy text editor, sort of the way one can now navigate a Macintosh computer— or a commercial online service such as Prodigy.

Then there are the Internet services themselves.

For every database now available through the Internet, there are probably three or four that are not. Government agencies are only now beginning to connect their storehouses of information to the Net. Several commercial vendors, from database services to booksellers, have made their services available through the Net.

Few people now use one of the Net's more interesting applications. A standard known as MIME lets one send audio and graphics files in a message. Imagine opening your e-mail one day to hear your grand-daughter's first words, or a "photo" of your friend's new house. Eventually, this standard could allow for distribution of even small video displays over the Net.

All of this will require vast new amounts of Net power, to handle both the millions of new people who will jump onto the Net and the new applications they want. Replicating a moving image on a com-puter screen alone takes a phenomenal amount of computer bits, and computing power to arrange them.

All of this combines into a National Information Infrastructure able to move billions of bits of information in one second—the kind of power needed to hook information "hoses" into every business and house.

As these "superhighways" grow, so will the "on ramps," for a high-speed road does you little good if you can't get to it. The costs of modems seem to fall as fast as those of computers. High-speed modems (9600 baud and up) are becoming increasingly affordable. At 9600 baud, you can download a satellite weather image of North America in less than two minutes, a file that with a slower modem could take up to 20 minutes to download. Eventually, homes could be connected directly to a national digital network. Most long-distance phone traffic is already carried in digital form, through high-volume optical fibers. Phone companies are ever so slowly working to extend these fibers the "final mile" to the home. The Electronic Frontier Foundation is working to ensure these links are affordable.

Beyond the technical questions are increasingly thorny social, politi-cal, and economic issues. Who is to have access to these services, and at what cost? If we live in an information age, are we laying the seeds for a new information underclass, unable to compete with those fortunate enough to have the money and skills needed to manipulate new communications channels? Who, in fact, decides who has access to what? As more companies realize the potential profits to be made in the new information infrastructure, what happens to such systems as Usenet, possibly the world's first successful anarchistic system, where everybody can say whatever they want?

What are the laws of the electronic frontier? When national and state boundaries lose their meaning in cyberspace, the question might even be: WHO is the law? What if a practice that is legal in one country is "committed" in another country where it is illegal, over a computer network that crosses through a third country? Who goes after computer crackers?

What role will you play in the revolution?

Appendix A
The Lingo

Like any community, the Net has developed its own language. What follows is a glossary of some of the more common phrases you'll likely run into. But it's only a small subset of net.speak. You an find a more complete listing in *The New Hacker's Dictionary*, compiled by Eric Raymond (MIT Press). Raymond's work is based on an online reference known as "The Jargon File," which you can get through anonymous ftp from ftp.gnu.mit.ai.mit as jarg300.txt.gz in the pub/gnu directory (see chapter 7 for information on how to uncompress a .gz file).

ANSI
Computers use several different methods for deciding how to put information on your screen and how your keyboard interacts with the screen. ANSI is one of these "terminal emulation" methods. Although most popular on PC-based bulletin board systems, it can also be found on some Net sites. To use it properly, you will first have to turn it on, or enable it, in your communications software.

ARPANet
A predecessor of the Internet. Started in 1969 with funds from the Defense Department's Advanced Projects Research Agency.

ASCII
Has two meanings. ASCII is a universal computer code for English letters and characters. Computers store all information as binary numbers. In ASCII, the letter *A* is stored as 01000001, whether the computer is made by IBM, Apple, or Commodore. ASCII also refers to a method, or protocol, for

copying files from one computer to another over a network, in which neither computer checks for any errors that might have been caused by static or other problems.

Backbone

A high-speed network that connects several powerful computers. In the United States, the backbone of the Internet is often considered the NSFNet, a government-funded link between a handful of supercomputer sites across the country.

Baud

The speed at which modems transfer data. One baud is roughly equal to one bit per second. It takes eight bits to make up one letter or character. Modems rarely transfer data at exactly the same speed as their listed baud rate because of static or computer problems. More expensive modems use systems, such as Microcom Network Protocol (MNP), that can correct for these errors or which "compress" data to speed up transmission.

BITNet

Another, academically oriented, international computer network, which uses a different set of computer instructions to move data. It is easily accessible to Internet users through e-mail, and provides a large number of conferences and databases. Its name comes from "Because It's Time."

Bounce

What your e-mail does when it cannot get to its recipient—it bounces back to you—unless it goes off into the ether, never to be found again.

Command line

On Unix host systems, this is where you tell the machine what you want it to do, by typing commands.

Communications software

A program that tells a modem how to work.

Daemon	An otherwise harmless Unix program that normally works out of sight of the user. On the Internet, you'll likely encounter it only when your e-mail is not delivered to your recipient—you'll get back your original message plus an ugly message from a "mailer daemon."
Distribution	A way to limit where your Usenet postings go. Handy for such things as "for sale" messages or discussions of regional politics.
Domain	The last part of an Internet address, such as "news.com."
Dot	When you want to impress the net veterans you meet at parties, say "dot" instead of "period," for example: "My address is john at site dot domain dot com."
Dot file	A file on a Unix public-access system that alters the way you or your messages interact with that system. For example, your .login file contains various parameters for such things as the text editor you get when you write a message. When you do an ls command, these files do not appear in the directory listing; do ls -a to list them.
Down	When a public-access site runs into technical trouble, and you can no longer gain access to it, it's down.
Download	Copy a file from a host system to your computer. There are several different methods, or protocols, for downloading files, most of which periodically check the file as it is being copied to ensure no information is inadvertently destroyed or damaged during the process. Some, such as XMODEM, let you download only one file at a time. Others, such as batch-YMODEM and ZMODEM, let you type in the names of several files at once, which are then automatically downloaded.

EMACS	A standard Unix text editor preferred by Unix types that beginners tend to hate.
E-mail	Electronic mail—a way to send a private message to somebody else on the Net. Used as both noun and verb.
Emoticon	See Smiley.
FAQ	Frequently Asked Questions. A compilation of answers to these. Many Usenet newsgroups have these files, which are posted once a month or so for beginners.
Film at 11	One reaction to an overwrought argument: "Imminent death of the Net predicted. Film at 11."
Finger	An Internet program that lets you get some bit of information about other users, provided they have first created a .plan file (see also .plan file).
Flame	Online yelling and/or ranting directed at somebody else. Often results in flame wars, which occasionally turn into holy wars (see also Holy war).
Followup	A Usenet posting that is a response to an earlier message.
Foo/foobar	A sort of online algebraic place holder, for example: "If you want to know whether a site is run by a for- profit company, look for an address in the form of foo@foobar.com."
Fortune cookie	An inane/witty/profound comment that can be found around the Net.
Freeware	Software that doesn't cost anything.
FTP	File-Transfer Protocol. A system for transferring files across the Net.
F2F	Face to Face. When you actually meet those people you've been corresponding with/flaming.

Get a life	What to say to somebody who has, perhaps, been spending a wee bit too much time in front of a computer.
GIF	Graphic Interchange Format. A format developed in the mid-1980s by CompuServe for use in photo-quality graphics images. Now commonly used everywhere online.
GNU	Gnu's Not Unix. A project of the Free Software Foundation to write a free version of the Unix operating system.
Hacker	On the Net, unlike among the general public, this is not a bad person; it simply refers to people who enjoy stretching hardware and software to their limits, seeing just what they can get their computers to do. What many people call hackers, net.denizens refer to as crackers.
Handshake	Two modems trying to connect first do this to agree on how to transfer data.
Hang	When a modem fails to hang up.
Holy war	Arguments that involve certain basic tenets of faith, about which one cannot disagree without setting one of these off. For example: IBM PCs are inherently superior to Macintoshes.
Host system	A public-access site; provides Net access to people outside the research and government community.
IMHO	In My Humble Opinion.
Internet	A worldwide system for linking smaller computer networks together. Networks connected through the Internet use a particular set of communications standards to communicate, known as TCP/IP (see also TCP/IP).
Killfile	A file that lets you filter Usenet postings to some extent, by excluding messages on certain topics or from certain people.
Log off	Disconnect from a host system.

Log on/log in	Connect to a host system or public-access site.
Lurk	Read messages in a Usenet newsgroup without ever saying anything.
Mailing list	Essentially a conference in which messages are delivered right to your mailbox, instead of to a Usenet newsgroup. You get on these by sending a message to a specific e- mail address, which is often that of a computer that automates the process.
MOTSS	Members Of The Same Sex. Gays and Lesbians online. Originally an acronym used in the 1980 federal census.
Net.god	One who has been online since the beginning, who knows all and who has done it all.
Netiquette	A set of commonsense guidelines for not annoying others.
Net.personality	Somebody sufficiently opinionated/flaky/with plenty of time to regularly post in dozens of different Usenet newsgroups, therefore someone whose presence is known to thousands of people.
Net.police	Derogatory term for those who would impose their standards on other users of the Net. Often used in flame wars (in which it occasionally mutates to net.nazis).
Network	A communications system that links two or more computers. It can be as simple as a cable strung between two computers a few feet apart or as complex as hundreds of thousands of computers around the world linked through fiber-optic cables, phone lines, and satellites.
Newbie	Somebody new to the Net. Sometimes used derogatorily by net veterans who have forgotten that, they, too, were once newbies who did not innately know the answer to everything. "Clueless newbie" is always derogatory.

Newsgroup	A Usenet conference.
NIC	Network Information Center. As close as an Internet- style network gets to a hub; it's usually where you'll find information about that particular network.
NSA line eater	The more aware/paranoid Net users believe that the National Security Agency has a superpowerful computer assigned to reading everything posted on the Net. They will jokingly (?) refer to this line eater in their postings. Goes back to the early days of the Net when the bottom lines of messages would sometimes disappear for no apparent reason.
NSF	National Science Foundation. Funds the NSFNet, a high-speed network that once formed the backbone of the Internet in the United States.
Offline	When your computer is not connected to a host system or the Net, you are offline.
Online	When your computer is connected to an online service, bulletin board system, or public-access site.
Ping	A program that can trace the route a message takes from your site to another site.
.plan file	A file that lists anything you want others on the Net to know about you. You place it in your home directory on your public-access site. Then, anybody who fingers you will get to see this file (see also Finger).
Post	To compose a message for a Usenet newsgroup and then send it out for others to see.
Postmaster	The person to contact at a particular site to ask for information about the site or complain about a user's behavior.

Prompt

When the host system asks you to do something and waits for you to respond. For example, if you see the "login:" prompt, it means type your user name.

Protocol

The method used to transfer a file between a host system and your computer. There are several types, such as Kermit, YMODEM, and ZMODEM.

README files

Files found on ftp sites that explain what is in a given ftp directory or which provide other useful information (such as how to use ftp).

Real Soon Now

A vague term used to describe when something will allegedly happen.

RFC

Request For Comments. A series of documents that describe various technical aspects of the Internet.

ROTFL

Rolling On The Floor Laughing. How to respond to a particularly funny comment.

ROT13

A simple way to encode bad jokes, movie reviews that give away the ending, pornography, etc. Essentially, each letter in a message is replaced by the letter 13 spaces away from it in the alphabet. There are online decoders to read these; nn and rn have them built in.

RTFM

Read The, uh, you know, Manual. Often used in flames against people who ask computer-related questions that could be easily answered with a few minutes with a manual. More politely: RTM.

Screen capture

A part of your communications software that opens a file on your computer and saves to it whatever scrolls past on the screen while you are connected to a host system.

Server

A computer that can distribute information or files automatically in response to specifically worded e-mail requests.

Shareware	Software that is freely available on the Net. If you like and use the software, you should send in the fee requested by the author, whose name and address will be found in a file distributed with the software.
.sig file	Sometimes, .signature file. A file that, when placed in your home directory on your public-access site, will automatically be appended to every Usenet posting you write.
Signal-to-noise ratio	The amount of useful information to be found in a given Usenet newsgroup. Often used derogatorily, for example: "the signal-to-noise ratio in this newsgroup is pretty low."
.sig quote	A profound/witty/quizzical/whatever quote that you include in your .sig file.
SIMTEL20	The White Sands Missile Range used to maintain a giant collection of free and low-cost software of all kinds, which was "mirrored" to numerous other ftp sites on the Net. In the fall of 1993, the Air Force decided it had better things to do than maintain a free software library and shut it down. But you'll still see references to the collection, known as SIMTEL20, around the Net.
Smiley	A way to describe emotion online. Look at this with your head tilted to the left :-). There are scores of these smileys, from grumpy to quizzical.
Snail mail	Mail that comes through a slot in your front door or a box mounted outside your house.
Sysadmin	The system administrator; the person who runs a host system or public-access site.
Sysop	A system operator. Somebody who runs a bulletin board system.
TANSTAAFL	There Ain't No Such Thing As A Free Lunch.

TCP/IP	Transmission Control Protocol/Internet Protocol. The particular system for transferring information over a computer network that is at the heart of the Internet.
Telnet	A program that lets you connect to other computers on the Internet.
Terminal emulation	There are several methods for determining how your keystrokes and screen interact with a public-access site's operating system. Most communications programs offer a choice of "emulations" that let you mimic the keyboard that would normally be attached directly to the host-system computer.
Upload	Copy a file from your computer to a host system.
User name	On most host systems, the first time you connect you are asked to supply a one-word user name. This can be any combination of letters and numbers.
UUCP	Unix-to-Unix CoPy. A method for transferring Usenet postings and e-mail that requires far fewer net resources than TCP/IP, but which can result in considerably slower transfer times.
VT100	Another terminal emulation system. Supported by many communications programs, it is the most common one in use on the Net. VT102 is a newer version.

Appendix B
Electronic Frontier
Foundation Information

The Electronic Frontier Foundation (EFF) is a membership organization that was founded in July 1990 to ensure that the principles embodied in the Constitution and the Bill of Rights are protected as new communications technologies emerge.

From the beginning, EFF has worked to shape our nation's communications infrastructure and the policies that govern it in order to maintain and enhance First Amendment, privacy, and other democratic values. We believe that our overriding public goal must be the creation of Electronic Democracy, so our work focuses on the establishment of

• new laws that protect citizens' basic Constitutional rights as they use new communications technologies,

• a policy of common carriage requirements for all network providers so that all speech, no matter how controversial, will be carried without discrimination,

• a National Public Network where voice, data, and video services are accessible to all citizens on an equitable and affordable basis, and

• a diversity of communities that enable all citizens to have a voice in the information age.

Join Us!

I wish to become a member of the Electronic Frontier Foundation. I enclose:

$_____ Regular membership—$40

$_____ Student membership—$20

Special Contribution

I wish to make a tax-deductible donation in the amount of $_____
to further support the activities of EFF and to broaden participation
in the organization.

Documents Available in Hard-Copy Form

The following documents are available free of charge from the Electronic Frontier Foundation. Please indicate any of the documents you
wish to receive.

____ *Open Platform Proposal*—EFF's proposal for a national telecommunications infrastructure. 12 pages. July 1992.

____ *An Analysis of the FBI Digital Telephony Proposal*—Response of
EFF-organized coalition to the FBI's digital telephony proposal of Fall
1992. 8 pages. September 1992.

____ *Building the Open Road: The NREN and the National Public Network*—
A discussion of the National Research and Education Network as a
prototype for a National Public Network. 20 pages. May 1992.

____ *Innovative Services Delivered Now: ISDN Applications at Home, School,
the Workplace and Beyond*—A compilation of ISDN applications currently in use. 29 pages. January 1993.

____ *Decrypting the Puzzle Palace*—John Perry Barlow's argument for
strong encryption and the need for an end to U.S. policies preventing
its development and use. 13 pages. May 1992.

____ *Crime and Puzzlement*—John Perry Barlow's piece on the founding
of the Electronic Frontier Foundation and the world of hackers, crackers, and those accused of computer crimes. 24 pages. June 1990.

____ *Networks & Policy*—A quarterly newsletter detailing EFF's activities
and achievements.

Your Contact Information

Name: _____

Organization: _____

Address: _____

_____

Phone: (____) _____ FAX: (____) _____ (optional)

E-mail address: _____

Payment Method

____ Enclosed is a check payable to the Electronic Frontier Foundation.

____ Please charge my

____ MasterCard ____ Visa ____ American Express

Card Number: _____

Expiration Date: _____

Signature: _____

Privacy Policy

EFF occasionally shares its mailing list with other organizations promoting similar goals. However, we respect an individual's right to privacy and will not distribute your name without explicit permission.

____ I grant permission for the EFF to distribute my name and contact information to organizations sharing similar goals.

Print out and mail to:

Membership Coordinator
Electronic Frontier Foundation
1001 G Street, N.W.
Suite 950 East
Washington, DC 20001
202/347–5400 voice
202/393–5509 fax

The Electronic Frontier Foundation is a nonprofit, 501(c)(3) organization supported by contributions from individual members, corporations, and private foundations. Donations are tax-deductible.

Index

$14.95
Computers/Networks

Everybody's Guide to the Internet
Adam Gaffin
foreword by Mitchell Kapor

If you have access to a <u>personal computer and want to explore the</u>
Internet, Everybody's Guide is the place to begin.

Everybody's Guide is designed to make you comfortable in the virtual world of the Internet with its insider language and peculiar local
culture. Accessible, friendly, and authoritative, it offers a clear, bare-
bones introduction to the Internet, with just enough technical information to get you online. Additional help is offered at the end of each
chapter in the form of a section on what to do "when things go
wrong," and another section, called "FYI," tells you where to look for
further information.

Everybody's Guide covers everything you need to know about the
rich and complex Internet environment: e-mail (including advanced e-
mail); the "global watering hole" called Usenet and its essential newsgroups; mailing lists and bitnet; bulletin board systems; downloading
files via ftp; information utilities such as telnet, gopher, archie, veronica, WAIS, and the World-Wide Web; information services such as
library catalogs, weather reports, and travel advisories; news services;
IRC and MUDs; and the network in the classroom.

Adam Gaffin is a Senior Writer at Network World.

The Internet is growing and changing so quickly that to help keep
users up to date, Everybody's Update to the Internet is posted monthly and is available for free online over the Internet.

Everybody's Guide was originally "published" electronically as The
Big Dummy's Guide to the Internet. It is sponsored by the Electronic
Frontier Foundation, a nonprofit organization founded by Mitchell
Kapor and John Perry Barlow that works to protect civil liberties in
emerging technologies.

The MIT Press
Massachusetts Institute of Technology
Cambridge, Massachusetts 02142

GAFBP 0-262-57105-6

jacket design by Jean Wilcox

90000

9 780262 671057